Julie Stafford's Low Cholesterol Cookbook

Conquer cholesterol
the **Taste of Life** way

Viking

Published by the Penguin Group
Penguin Books Australia Ltd
487 Maroondah Highway, PO Box 257
Ringwood, Victoria 3134, Australia
Penguin Books Ltd
80 Strand, London WC2R 0RL, England
Penguin Putnam Inc.
375 Hudson Street, New York, New York 10014, USA
Penguin Books Canada Limited
10 Alcorn Avenue, Toronto, Ontario, Canada M4V 3B2
Penguin Books (NZ) Ltd
Cnr Rosedale and Airborne Roads, Albany, Auckland, New Zealand
Penguin Books (South Africa) (Pty) Ltd
24 Sturdee Avenue, Rosebank, Johannesburg 2196, South Africa
Penguin Books India (P) Ltd
11, Community Centre, Panchsheel Park, New Delhi 110 017, India

First published by Penguin Books Australia Ltd 1991
This edition published 1997

14 13 12 11 10 9 8 7 6

Photography by Mark Chew
Food preparation and styling by Fiona Hammond
Illustrations by Cathy Larsen
Typeset in 12/14 pt Bembo by Midland Typesetters, Maryborough, Victoria
Printed in Australia by McPherson's Printing Group, Maryborough, Victoria

National Library of Australia
Cataloguing-in-Publication data:

Stafford, Julie.
  Julie Stafford's low cholesterol cookbook.

  {New ed.}.
  Includes index.
  ISBN 0 670 87577 5.

  1. Low-cholesterol diet – Recipes. I. Title.
  II. Title: Low cholesterol cookbook.

641.5638

www.penguin.com.au

Front cover photograph

Chicken and Eggplant Lasagne Slice (see page 72) with Broccoli, Cauliflower, Tomato and Pine Nut Salad (see page 46).

Contents

Introduction

Cholesterol is an organic chemical compound – a sterol. It is wax-like, almost fatty in appearance and touch, and does not dissolve in water or blood. Every day our bodies produce about one gram of cholesterol naturally, yet the body does not require all the cholesterol that it makes. The manufacturing of this cholesterol takes place in the liver, but almost every cell in our body has the capacity to make cholesterol for itself.

The function of cholesterol is to make hormones, bile and cell membranes, so it is essential for good health. However, too much cholesterol in the blood means that it builds up on the artery walls, resulting in the artery-narrowing disease called atherosclerosis. Atherosclerosis appears to be a precursor to heart disease and stroke.

Because our diets are high in cholesterol-rich foods and saturated fats we end up with approximately four times more cholesterol per day than we require. Some of this will be used for hormones, some used to make cell membranes and bile,

and some will be excreted. But over a period of years the excess cholesterol will slowly build up inside the arteries, narrowing them, which will disturb the blood flow to vital organs in the body and put extra pressure on the heart, as it has to pump harder and harder to maintain a good flow of blood and oxygen throughout the body.

Cholesterol in the blood is differentiated into two kinds and referred to as high density lipoprotein (HDL) or low density lipoprotein (LDL). HDL is the 'good' cholesterol. It is thought that this cholesterol actually helps to remove all cholesterol from the blood and therefore protect against heart disease. LDL is the 'bad' cholesterol because it is thought that it contributes to the build-up of fatty substances on the artery walls.

Saturated fats are our biggest dietary problem, because they tend to raise the LDL and lower the HDL. Saturated fat foods include fatty meats, processed fast foods, solid cooking oils, butter, some margarines, full cream milk, cream, yoghurt, full fat cheese, chocolate and coconut oil.

Recent studies indicate that polyunsaturated fats tend to lower the amount of both LDL and HDL. Polyunsaturated foods include some margarines, nuts, safflower and sunflower oil, fish, shellfish, seeds and grapeseed oil.

Mono-unsaturated fats tend to lower the LDL but increase the HDL. Mono-unsaturated foods include olive oil and olives, avocado, chicken, tuna and salmon.

Fish contains Omega 3 fatty acid, which studies now show plays an important role in the protection against LDL cholesterol. It appears that the Omega 3 fatty acid actually raises the level of the good, HDL cholesterol in the blood. Omega 3 fatty acid also helps to make the blood thinner, less sticky, less likely to clot and reduces platelet clumping.

This book looks at the foods that may help us to lower our blood cholesterol levels and reduce the risk of heart disease. The recipes are all designed to promote foods that are low in saturated fat, low in cholesterol, have no added salt or sugar and are high in fibre, especially soluble fibre. The recipes also aim to increase our overall intake of vitamin C and calcium by including foods that are high in these nutrients. While this may not guarantee a lowering of blood cholesterol level for everyone, the recipes in this book can also help you to lose weight and increase your energy levels. They can assist your immune system to function healthily, and should supply your body with the nutrients it needs to protect itself against many other everyday illnesses.

Here's to your health!

Cooking techniques for low cholesterol cooking

The following cooking techniques avoid increasing the fat and cholesterol levels of our food, while preserving its goodness.

STIR-FRYING BECOMES DRY-STIR-FRYING

This technique requires a non-stick surface or a good quality stainless steel pan. To prepare the surface of these pans, pour in a little cold pressed oil. Use a tissue to distribute the oil evenly over base and sides. Wipe out any excess oil. Heat the pan and add ingredients, tossing over the hot surface continually. Do not have temperature as high as you would if you were using oil. Cook the ingredients with the strongest flavours first, like garlic, ginger and onions. If you are using spices, these can be added with the onions. If the pan begins to smoke, you have the temperature too high.

Place the lid on vegetables for 30 seconds when they are nearly done to ensure bright, vibrant colours.

SIMMERING

Food should not be completely covered with liquid and the heat should be kept low. First bring to near boiling, then turn down so the liquid gently bubbles.

STEAMING

Food is placed above simmering water, creating hot steam that cooks the food. Food can also be steamed over stock or vegetable juices. You can add herbs to the liquid too, which will flavour the food being steamed.

DRY BAKING

Excellent results can be achieved by placing vegetables on a tray lined with non-stick baking paper, and cooking in a hot oven. The vegetables do not need to be turned. They are crisp and crunchy on the outside and super-moist on the inside. This is especially good for potatoes.

BLANCHING

Drop vegetables into a pan of rapidly boiling water for a few minutes only. This brings out the vibrant colours of vegetables while they hold their texture and retain their nutrients.

MICROWAVING

You simply just don't need oil to cook in a microwave oven. Foods cook in their own natural juices. Microwaving seals in the nutrients so is considered an excellent way to cook vegetables, fish and chicken.

'OIL' COOKING

Some recipes use 1–2 teaspoons of (light) olive oil in their cooking. If you do not wish to use oil, simply substitute 1 tablespoon of water and follow the same cooking procedure. This very small amount of oil is used to enhance the flavour of the ingredients used. Keep heat down on low and toss ingredients through the oil. Then cover and cook slowly and gently for best results.

The
Low Cholesterol
Breakfast

Breakfast in a Glass

1 cup low-fat milk or low-fat
  soymilk
1–2 teaspoons vanilla essence
2–4 dates, stones removed
1 banana or apple, peeled and
  cored
2 teaspoons oat bran

Put all ingredients in a blender and
blend until smooth and thick.
Drink immediately.

Apple, Celery and Ginger Juice

300 g apples, cored
50 g celery
small piece fresh ginger

Place apples, celery and ginger in
juicer and juice.

Apple and Cucumber Juice

300 g apples, cored
100 g cucumber, peeled

Place apples and cucumber in juicer
and juice.

Apple and Grape Juice

200 g apples, cored
150 g grapes

Place apples and grapes in juicer
and juice.

Apple and Lemon Juice

300 g apples, cored
¼ cup freshly squeezed lemon juice

Place apples in juicer and juice. Mix apple and lemon juice together.

Apricot Juice

350–400 g apricots, stones removed

Place apricots in juicer and juice.

(Apricot juice is a meal all on its own. It is a delicious thick purée, full of goodness. You may prefer to thin it down with water, fresh orange, mango, grape or apple juice. It combines well with all of these, and passionfruit pulp gives it a nice bite.)

Carrot Juice

350 g carrots

Place carrots in juicer and juice.

Carrot and Celery Juice

SERVES 1

300 g carrots
50 g celery

Place carrots and celery in juicer and juice.

Carrot, Celery and Ginger Juice

SERVES 1

300 g carrots
50 g celery
piece of fresh ginger (the size of
  a large marble)

Place carrots, celery and ginger in juicer and juice.

(This makes an excellent breakfast juice to start the day.)

Grape Juice

SERVES 1

300–350 g green or purple grapes

Place grapes in juicer and juice.

(Grape juice combines well with nearly all other fruit juices so enjoy making up your own combinations.)

Grapefruit and Orange Juice

SERVES I

1 medium-sized grapefruit
2 medium-sized oranges

Place grapefruit and oranges in juicer and juice.

Green Juice

any combinations of the following:
lettuce, spinach, a little cabbage,
parsley, kale, wild carrot tops,
radish tops, cress, wheat grass,
alfalfa sprouts, comfrey,
cucumber, celery and especially
celery foliage

Place your selection of green vegetables in juicer and juice.

(This juice can also be added to others like carrot, celery or beetroot juice.)

Lemon Zinger Juice

SERVES I

¼–½ cup freshly squeezed lemon
juice
½–¾ cup pure mineral spring
water

Mix together juice and water.

Tomato Juice

SERVES I

350 g ripe tomatoes

Place tomatoes in juicer and juice.

(Tomato juice combines well with carrot and cucumber juice. You can also add crushed garlic or crushed fresh ginger, for a different flavour.)

Watermelon Juice

SERVES I

350 g watermelon, seeds removed

Place watermelon in juicer and juice.

Oat Bran Porridge

SERVES I

⅓ cup oat bran
I cup water

Place bran and water in a saucepan and slowly bring to the boil, stirring continuously. Turn heat right down, cover and cook until it reaches desired consistency.

Oat Bran and Oatmeal Porridge

¼ cup oatmeal
2 tablespoons oat bran
1 cup water

Place ingredients in a saucepan and slowly bring to the boil, stirring continuously. Turn heat right down, cover and cook until it reaches desired consistency.

SERVING SUGGESTIONS

- Add a couple of drops of vanilla essence or some grated orange and lemon rind for added flavour instead of salt.
- Slow cooking will create a moist porridge and it is not necessary to add a serving liquid. However, if you do, you might like to try low-fat milk or low-fat soymilk, or fruit juice.
- Add your favourite fresh seasonal fruit to make a complete meal, like strawberries, banana, kiwi fruit, mango or papaw.

Apple and Sultana Muffins

2 cups oat bran
2 cups unbleached wholemeal flour
6 teaspoons baking powder
2 teaspoons ground cinnamon
1 teaspoon mixed spice
6 medium-sized Granny Smith
  apples
boiling water
1 cup sultanas
grated rind of 1 lemon
½ cup apple juice concentrate
½ cup cold pressed grapeseed oil
¾ cup unsweetened orange juice
¼ cup lemon juice
3 egg whites

Preheat oven to 180°C.

Place oat bran in a large bowl. Combine wholemeal flour, baking powder and spices and sift over the oat bran.

Peel and core apples, dice and cover with boiling water. Stand for 5 minutes. Drain. Add apples, sultanas and lemon rind to the flour and oat mixture. Mix well to coat with flour.

Combine apple juice concentrate, oil, orange and lemon juice and add to the flour and apple mixture.

Beat egg whites just lightly and gently add to the mixture. Spoon into lightly oiled and floured or 'oat branned' muffin tray, and bake in oven for 25–30 minutes.

Remove muffins from the tray and place on a wire rack to cool. Cover with a tea towel.

Banana, Carob and Clove Muffins

2 cups oat bran
2 cups unbleached wholemeal flour
¼ cup carob powder
6 teaspoons baking powder
1 teaspoon mixed spice
½ teaspoon ground cloves
400 g ripe bananas, mashed
1 cup low-fat milk or low-fat
  soymilk
½ cup apple juice concentrate
½ cup cold pressed grapeseed oil
2 teaspoons vanilla essence
3 egg whites
12 walnuts (optional)

Preheat oven to 180°C.

Place oat bran in a bowl. Sift flour, carob, baking powder and spices over the oat bran and mix well.

In a large bowl combine banana, milk, apple juice concentrate, oil and vanilla essence and mix well. Add flour and oats to this mixture in two lots, mixing well with each addition.

Beat egg whites just lightly and add gently. Spoon the mixture into lightly oiled and 'oat branned' muffin tray. The mixture will come up over the top of the tray. Decorate with walnuts. Bake for 25–30 minutes.

Remove muffins from the tray and place on a wire rack to cool. Cover with a tea towel.

Banana and Date Muffins

2½ cups oat bran
1½ cups unbleached wholemeal
  flour
6 teaspoons baking powder
2 teaspoons mixed spice
1 teaspoon ground cinnamon
500 g finely chopped banana
100 g finely chopped dates
½ cup apple juice concentrate
½ cup cold pressed grapeseed oil
1 cup low-fat evaporated skim milk
3 egg whites

Preheat oven to 180°C.

Place oat bran in a large bowl. Sift flour, baking powder and spices over the oat bran. Mix through with hands. Add banana and dates and toss well to break up and coat with flour mixture.

Combine apple juice concentrate, grapeseed oil and milk and mix into the flour and oat mixture.

Beat egg whites until stiff and gently fold them through the muffin mixture. Spoon into lightly oiled and 'oat branned' muffin tray. The mixture will come up over the top of tray. Cook for 25–30 minutes.

Remove muffins from the tray and place on a wire rack to cool. Cover with a tea towel.

Blueberry Oat Muffins

2 cups oat bran
2 cups unbleached white flour
6 teaspoons baking powder
1 teaspoon ground cinnamon
1 teaspoon mixed spice
½ teaspoon ground ginger
400 g blueberries (fresh or frozen,
   not canned)
½ cup cold pressed grapeseed oil
½ cup apple juice concentrate
1 cup non-fat or low-fat buttermilk
2 teaspoons vanilla essence
3 egg whites

Preheat oven to 180°C.

Place oat bran in a large bowl. Sift flour, baking powder, cinnamon, mixed spice and ginger over the oat bran, and mix through. Add the blueberries and coat well with flour.

Combine oil, apple juice concentrate, buttermilk and vanilla and fold into the flour and fruit mixture. Try not to squash the blueberries.

Beat egg whites until stiff and gently fold them through the muffin mixture. Spoon into lightly oiled and floured muffin tray. Bake for 25–30 minutes.

Remove muffins from the tray immediately and place on a wire rack to cool. Cover with a tea towel.

Blueberry and Pineapple Muffins

MAKES 12 LARGE MUFFINS

2 cups oat bran
2 cups unbleached white flour
6 teaspoons baking powder
1 teaspoon ground cinnamon
1 teaspoon mixed spice
1 teaspoon ground ginger
1 × 440 g can unsweetened pineapple pieces, well drained
200 g blueberries (fresh or frozen, not canned)
¾ cup unsweetened pineapple juice (reserved from canned pineapple)
¼ cup water
½ cup apple juice concentrate
½ cup cold pressed grapeseed oil
2 teaspoons vanilla essence
3 egg whites

Preheat oven to 180°C.

Place oat bran in a large bowl. Sift flour, baking powder and spices over oat bran and mix through.

Drain pineapple, reserving the juice. Chop up the pineapple pieces and add them, with the blueberries, to the bowl. Mix thoroughly so the fruit is coated well with flour mixture.

Combine reserved pineapple juice, water, apple juice concentrate, oil and vanilla essence. Add to the flour and fruit mixture and fold through.

Beat egg whites until stiff and gently fold them through the muffin mixture. Spoon into lightly oiled and floured muffin tray. Bake for 25–30 minutes.

Remove muffins from the tray and place on a wire rack to cool. Cover with a tea towel.

Carrot and Ginger Muffins

2 cups oat bran
I cup rolled oats
I cup unbleached white flour
6 teaspoons baking powder
400 g carrots
125 g glacé ginger, chopped
100 g dried apricots, chopped
½ cup apple juice concentrate
½ cup cold pressed grapeseed oil
grated rind of 2 lemons
4 egg whites

Preheat oven to 180°C.

Combine oat bran and rolled oats in a medium-sized bowl. Sift flour and baking powder over oats and mix through.

Juice carrots in a juicer, giving you approximately 150 g carrot pulp and 1 cup of juice. Combine the carrot pulp and juice with remaining ingredients, except egg whites, in a large bowl. Add the flour and oat mixture in three lots, stirring well each time.

Beat egg whites until stiff and gently fold them through the muffin mixture. Spoon into lightly oiled and 'oat branned' muffin tray. The mixture will come up over the top of the tray. Bake for 25–30 minutes.

Remove muffins from the tray and place on a wire rack to cool. Cover with a tea towel.

Carrot and Mixed Peel Muffins

MAKES 12 LARGE MUFFINS

2 cups oat bran
2 cups unbleached white flour
6 teaspoons baking powder
1 teaspoon ground cinnamon
1 teaspoon mixed spice
400 g carrots
200 g mixed peel
½ cup apple juice concentrate
½ cup cold pressed grapeseed oil
2 teaspoons vanilla essence
grated rind of 2 oranges
4 egg whites

Preheat oven to 180°C.

Place oat bran in a bowl. Sift flour, baking powder and spices over the oat bran and mix through.

Juice carrots in a juicer, giving you approximately 150 g carrot pulp and 1 cup of juice. In a large bowl combine carrot pulp, carrot juice, mixed peel, apple juice concentrate, oil, vanilla essence and orange rind and mix thoroughly. Add the flour and oat mixture in three lots, stirring well each time.

Beat egg whites until stiff and gently fold them through the muffin mixture. Spoon into lightly oiled and 'oat branned' muffin tray. The mixture will come up to the top of the tray. Bake for 25–30 minutes.

Remove muffins from the tray and place on a wire rack to cool. Cover with a tea towel.

Corn Meal and Currant
Bran Muffins

2 cups corn meal
2 cups oat bran
6 teaspoons baking powder
1 cup currants
1 cup non-fat or low-fat yoghurt
1 cup low-fat milk or low-fat
  soymilk
½ cup apple juice concentrate
½ cup cold pressed grapeseed oil
2 teaspoons vanilla essence
3 egg whites

Preheat oven to 180°C.

Combine corn meal, oat bran, baking powder and currants in a large bowl and mix well.

In another bowl combine all remaining ingredients, except egg whites, and add this liquid to the corn meal and oat mixture.

Beat egg whites lightly and fold through the muffin mixture. Spoon into lightly oiled and 'oat branned' muffin tray. Bake for 20–25 minutes.

Remove muffins from the tray and place on a wire rack to cool. Cover with a tea towel.

Fresh Pear and Cinnamon Muffins

MAKES 12 LARGE MUFFINS

1 cup rolled oats
2 cups oat bran
1 cup unbleached white flour
6 teaspoons baking powder
3 teaspoons ground cinnamon
¼ cup lemon juice
¾ cup unsweetened orange juice
½ cup apple juice concentrate
½ cup cold pressed grapeseed oil
2 teaspoons vanilla essence
400 g Packham pears, cored and diced
3 egg whites

Preheat oven to 180°C.

Combine rolled oats and oat bran. Sift flour, baking powder and cinnamon over the oats and combine.

Combine remaining ingredients, except egg whites, in a large bowl. Slowly fold the dry ingredients into the fruit juice liquid, mixing well until everything is combined.

Beat egg whites until stiff peaks form and gently fold through the mixture in the bowl. Spoon into lightly oiled and 'oat branned' muffin tray. The mixture will come up over the top of the tray. Bake for 25–30 minutes.

Remove muffins from the tray and place on a wire rack to cool. Cover with a tea towel.

Spicy Pear and Almond Muffins

MAKES 12 LARGE MUFFINS

2½–3 teaspoons Spice Mixture
(see below)
1 cup rolled oats
2 cups oat bran
1 cup unbleached white flour
6 teaspoons baking powder
500 g cooked pears or canned
unsweetened pears in natural
juice, well drained
grated rind of 1 lemon
½ cup apple juice concentrate
1 cup cooking liquid from pears or
unsweetened pear juice
(reserved from canned pears)
½ cup cold pressed grapeseed oil
2 teaspoons vanilla essence
3 egg whites
6 teaspoons ground almonds

SPICE MIXTURE
ground cinnamon
ground cloves
ground peppercorn powder
ground ginger
ground cardamom

Preheat oven to 180°C.

Make up spice mixture first.
Combine equal portions of all the
spices and mix well. This mixture
keeps well in an airtight container.

Combine rolled oats and oat bran
in a large bowl. Sift flour, baking
powder and spice mixture over the
oats.

Dice pears and combine with
lemon rind, apple juice concentrate,
pear juice, oil and vanilla, and add
to the flour and oat mixture,
mixing well.

Beat egg whites until stiff peaks
form and gently fold through the
mixture. Spoon into a lightly oiled
and 'oat branned' muffin tray.
Sprinkle ½ teaspoon of ground
almonds over the top of each
muffin. Bake for 25–30 minutes.

Remove muffins from the tray
immediately and place on a wire
rack to cool. Cover with a tea
towel.

Pineapple and Date Muffins MAKES 12 LARGE MUFFINS

2 cups oat bran
2 cups soy flour or unbleached
white flour
6 teaspoons baking powder
2 teaspoons ground cinnamon
2 × 440 g cans unsweetened
pineapple pieces, well drained
200 g chopped dates
1 cup unsweetened pineapple juice
(reserved from canned pineapple)
½ cup cold pressed grapeseed oil
½ cup apple juice concentrate
2 teaspoons vanilla essence
3 egg whites

Preheat oven to 180°C.

Place oat bran in a bowl. Sift flour, baking powder and cinnamon over oat bran and mix through.

Chop pineapple pieces and in a large bowl combine them with dates, pineapple juice, oil, apple juice concentrate and vanilla essence. Fold in the flour and oat bran mixture in three lots.

Beat egg whites until stiff and fold them through the muffin mixture. Spoon into lightly oiled and floured muffin tray and bake for 25–30 minutes.

Remove muffins from the tray immediately and place on a wire rack to cool. Cover with a tea towel.

Pumpkin and Prune Muffins MAKES 12 LARGE MUFFINS

500 g pumpkin
2 cups oat bran
¾ cup rolled oats
1¼ cups unbleached white flour
1 teaspoon ground cinnamon
1 teaspoon mixed spice
½ teaspoon ground nutmeg
6 teaspoons baking powder
200 g moist prunes, chopped
1 generous tablespoon grated
  lemon rind
1 cup unsweetened orange juice
½ cup apple juice concentrate
½ cup cold pressed grapeseed oil
1 teaspoon vanilla essence
3 egg whites

Preheat oven to 180°C.

Place pumpkin in a steamer and cook until tender. Drain well before mashing thoroughly.

Place oat bran and rolled oats in a large bowl. Sift flour, spices and baking powder over the oats and mix them through the mixture with your hands.

In another bowl combine pumpkin, prunes, lemon rind, orange juice, apple juice concentrate, oil and vanilla essence. Add this to the flour and oat mixture and mix well.

Beat egg whites until stiff and gently fold them through the muffin mixture. Spoon into lightly oiled and 'oat branned' muffin tray. The mixture will come up over the top of the tray. Bake for 25–30 minutes.

Remove muffins from the tray immediately and place on a wire rack to cool. Cover with a tea towel.

Rhubarb and Cinnamon Muffins

MAKES 12 LARGE MUFFINS

1 cup rolled oats
2 cups oat bran
1 cup unbleached white flour
6 teaspoons baking powder
1 teaspoon baking soda
2 teaspoons ground cinnamon
400 g rhubarb, chopped into small
    pieces
½ cup cold pressed grapeseed oil
½ cup apple juice concentrate
1 cup low-fat evaporated skim milk
2 teaspoons vanilla essence
4 egg whites

Preheat oven to 180°C.

Combine rolled oats and oat bran in a large bowl. Sift flour, baking powder, baking soda and cinnamon over the oats and mix through. Add rhubarb and coat well with flour.

Combine oil, apple juice concentrate, skim milk and vanilla, and add to the flour and oat mixture.

Beat egg whites until stiff peaks form and gently fold through the mixture. Spoon into lightly oiled and 'oat branned' muffin tray and bake for 25–30 minutes.

Remove muffins from the tray immediately and place on a wire rack to cool. Cover with a tea towel.

Oat Pancakes

1 cup rolled oats
½ cup oat bran
1 cup unbleached wholemeal flour
2 teaspoons baking powder
¼ cup apple juice concentrate
2 cups water
1 teaspoon vanilla essence
2 egg whites

Combine rolled oats and oat bran in a large bowl. Sift flour and baking powder over oats, returning husks to the mixture.

Mix together apple juice concentrate, water and vanilla and stir into the oat and flour mixture.

Beat egg whites until stiff and gently fold them through the mixture. Cook a little mixture in a lightly oiled non-stick pancake pan until browned. Turn pancake over and brown the other side. Repeat to make 6 pancakes.

SERVING SUGGESTIONS

- Roll pancake around a whole banana and serve with low-fat whipped ricotta cream (see page 98).
- Serve with a suitable sauce from those included in this section.
- Serve with fresh strawberries and low-fat yoghurt.
- Serve with your favourite fresh fruit or a combination of fruits.

Buckwheat, Orange and Oat Bran Pancakes

MAKES 6

¾ cup buckwheat flour
¾ cup oat bran
1 teaspoon baking powder
1 cup low-fat milk or low-fat
  soymilk
½ cup unsweetened orange juice
1 tablespoon apple juice
  concentrate
grated rind of 1 orange
2 egg whites

Place all ingredients in a food processor and purée until smooth. Pour a little mixture onto a lightly oiled hot pancake pan. Cook until lightly browned, then turn over and brown the other side. Repeat until all the mixture is used.

Corn Meal and Oat Bran Pancakes

MAKES 6

1 cup fine corn meal
½ cup oat bran
2 teaspoons baking powder
1 tablespoon cold pressed
  grapeseed oil
2 tablespoons apple juice
  concentrate
2 teaspoons vanilla essence
2 cups low-fat milk or low-fat
  soymilk
4 egg whites

Combine corn meal, oat bran and baking powder in a bowl and mix well.

Mix together oil, apple juice concentrate, vanilla and milk, and stir into the corn meal and oat mixture.

Beat egg whites until stiff and gently fold them through the mixture. Stand for 10 minutes, then mix well again. Spoon onto a lightly oiled non-stick pancake pan and cook until brown. Turn pancake over and brown the other side. Stir the mixture well between each pancake. Excellent served with fresh bananas and Lemon Sauce (see page 25).

Zucchini, Cheese and Oat Bran Pancakes

1 cup rolled oats
½ cup oat bran
1 cup unbleached white flour
2 teaspoons baking powder
2 cups grated zucchini (juice squeezed out), firmly packed
¼ cup low-fat grating cheese, firmly packed
1 cup low-fat evaporated skim milk
1 cup water
2 egg whites
black pepper to taste

Combine oats and oat bran in a large bowl. Sift flour and baking powder over the oats and combine. Add zucchini and cheese and mix well.

Combine milk and water and stir into the flour and zucchini mixture, mixing thoroughly.

Beat egg whites until stiff and gently fold them through the mixture. Cook a little mixture on a lightly oiled non-stick pancake pan until browned. Turn over to brown the other side. Repeat to make 8 pancakes.

SERVING SUGGESTIONS

- Top with avocado, alfalfa sprouts and low-fat Soymilk Mayonnaise (see page 51) and roll up.
- Top with lettuce, tomato, cucumber slices, tuna and horseradish mayonnaise (grate fresh horseradish into low-fat Soymilk Mayonnaise).
- Make up a basic White Sauce (see page 26) and add chopped cooked chicken, left-over fish, salmon or cooked vegetables and use as a filling.
- Top with Mushroom Sauce (see page 25).
- Top with Sweet Tomato Sauce (see page 26) or dry-fried tomato rings.

Apple Sauce

6 cooking apples, peeled, cored
  and sliced
½ lemon
I cup water
I tablespoon cornflour
I tablespoon water

Place apples, lemon and water in a
saucepan. Cover and cook until

apples are soft. Remove lemon.
Mix water and cornflour to make a
paste. Stir through the apple and
continue cooking and stirring until
sauce thickens. Serve hot or cold.

Store in an airtight container in the
refrigerator or freezer (this sauce
freezes quite well).

Blueberry Sauce

2 cups unsweetened pear juice or
  water
¼ cup cornflour
⅓ cup apple juice concentrate
450 g blueberries (fresh or frozen,
  not canned)
I tablespoon lemon juice

Mix ¼ cup of pear juice or water
with cornflour to make a paste.
Combine all other ingredients in a
small saucepan and slowly bring to
the boil. Add cornflour paste and
stir continuously until sauce
thickens. Remove from heat and
cool slightly. Pour over pancakes
and serve.

Refrigerate any left-over sauce. It
will keep for about 1 week.

VARIATION
■ To make raspberry sauce, simply
  substitute raspberries for
  blueberries.

Lemon Sauce

¾ cup freshly squeezed lemon juice
½ cup apple juice concentrate
½ teaspoon orange essence
grated rind of 1 orange
1¼ cups water
¼ cup cornflour

Combine lemon juice, apple juice concentrate, orange essence, rind, and 1 cup of the water in a small saucepan. Slowly bring to the boil. Mix remaining ¼ cup of water and cornflour to make a paste. Add this to the lemon mixture in the saucepan and stir continuously until sauce thickens. Remove from heat and cool slightly. Pour over pancakes and serve.

The sauce keeps well in the refrigerator for about 1 week. Reheat and add a little water for a pouring consistency.

VARIATION

■ To make orange sauce, simply substitute orange juice for lemon juice.

Mushroom Sauce

200 g sliced mushrooms
1 teaspoon light olive oil
¼ teaspoon dried dill
¼ teaspoon dried thyme
¾ cup low-fat milk or low-fat soymilk
1 tablespoon cornflour
1 tablespoon finely chopped fresh parsley

Cook mushroom in oil with dill and thyme until mushroom has softened and changed colour. Mix a little of the milk with cornflour to make a paste and add this to the remaining milk. Combine thoroughly and add to the mushrooms. Keep stirring until sauce thickens. Add parsley prior to serving.

Sweet Tomato Sauce

MAKES 2 CUPS

1 small onion, peeled and diced
1 teaspoon crushed garlic
1 teaspoon light olive oil or a little
  water
1 cup grated carrot or pumpkin
½ cup red wine
1 × 400 g can whole tomatoes in
  natural juice, salt-free
2 tablespoons tomato paste
½ tablespoon finely chopped fresh
  parsley

In a saucepan cook onion and garlic in the oil or a little water until onion is soft. Add carrot or pumpkin and cook until vegetable is soft. Add wine.

Chop tomatoes and add to the pan with their juice. Stir in tomato paste. Simmer for 20 minutes, stirring frequently. Add parsley prior to serving.

White Sauce

MAKES 1 CUP

1 cup low-fat milk or low-fat
  soymilk
2 tablespoons cornflour
black pepper to taste

Pour all but 2 tablespoons of the milk into a saucepan and bring to the boil. Mix cornflour with remaining milk until smooth. Just as bubbles appear in the milk prior to boiling, add cornflour paste and stir continuously until sauce thickens. Season with black pepper.

This white sauce can form the basis of an enormous variety of pancake fillings. Simply add such foods as chopped cooked chicken, left-over fish, canned salmon, your favourite cooked vegetables, fresh herbs or spices.

Apple Spread

220 g dried apples
3 cups unsweetened pineapple
  juice
½ lemon
2 teaspoons grated lemon rind
2 teaspoons ground cinnamon

Combine all ingredients in a large saucepan and simmer over a gentle heat until apples are soft. Remove lemon. Purée the mixture in a blender and pour into sterilised jars. When cool, seal and store in the refrigerator.

Apricot Fruit Spread

125 g dried apricots
90 g dried apples
60 g raisins
3½ cups unsweetened orange juice

Combine all ingredients in a large saucepan and simmer over a gentle heat until fruit is soft. Purée the mixture in a blender and pour into sterilised jars. When cool, seal and store in the refrigerator.

Fresh Apricot Spread

1 cup unsweetened apple and pear
  juice
1 cup unsweetened orange juice
½ cup apple juice concentrate
2 teaspoons agar powder
½–1 tablespoon lemon juice
400 g stoned fresh apricots,
  roughly chopped

Place all ingredients, except apricots, in a saucepan and slowly bring to the boil. Simmer for 5 minutes. Add apricots and simmer for a further 15–20 minutes. Remove from heat. Pour into sterilised jars and allow to cool before refrigerating.

Blueberry Jam Spread

1½ cups unsweetened pear juice
⅓ cup apple juice concentrate
1 tablespoon lemon juice
2 teaspoons agar powder
450 g blueberries (fresh or frozen, not canned)

Combine pear juice, apple juice concentrate, lemon juice and agar in a saucepan. Slowly bring to the boil, stirring to dissolve the agar. Boil for 5 minutes. Add blueberries and boil for another 10 minutes. Pour into sterilised jars and allow to cool. Keep refrigerated.

Cherry Spread

1 cup unsweetened orange juice
1 cup apple juice concentrate
1 tablespoon lemon juice
¼ teaspoon grated lemon rind
½ bar agar, cut into small pieces or 2 teaspoons agar powder
500 g stoned cherries (fresh or frozen, not canned)

Place all ingredients, except cherries, in a saucepan. Slowly bring to the boil. Simmer for 15 minutes, stirring occasionally. Add cherries and slowly bring to the boil again. Simmer for 5 minutes. Pour into sterilised jars, allow to cool, and refrigerate.

Raspberry Spread

1¼ cups unsweetened apple and
   pear juice
2 teaspoons agar powder
¼ cup apple juice concentrate
450 g raspberries (fresh or frozen,
   not canned)

Place apple and pear juice, agar and apple juice concentrate in a saucepan. Slowly bring to the boil and simmer for 5 minutes. Add raspberries and slowly bring to the boil again. Simmer for 5 minutes. Remove from heat. Pour into sterilised jars and allow to cool before refrigerating.

Strawberry Spread

2 cups unsweetened apple and
   pear juice or unsweetened
   orange juice
4 teaspoons agar powder
¾ cup apple juice concentrate
1 kg strawberries (fresh or frozen,
   not canned)

Place all ingredients, except strawberries, in a saucepan and slowly bring to the boil. Simmer for 5 minutes. Add strawberries and bring to the boil again. Simmer for 20–25 minutes. Remove from heat and pour into sterilised jars. Cool and refrigerate.

The
Low Cholesterol
Lunch

Alfalfa Sprouts, Celery, Walnuts and Fish Pitta

FILLS ½ PITTA

¼ cup cold, cooked, flaked fish
  fillet
¼ cup alfalfa sprouts
2 tablespoons thinly sliced celery
2–3 walnuts, roughly chopped
½ small wholemeal pitta bread

Combine all ingredients, and add a little dressing of your choice (see pages 49–51). Spoon into open pitta pocket.

Beetroot, Lettuce, Mushroom and Cucumber Pitta

FILLS ½ PITTA

¼ cup grated beetroot
¼ cup shredded lettuce
2–3 mushrooms, sliced
2–3 slices cucumber
½ small wholemeal pitta bread
a little freshly chopped dill
black pepper to taste

After grating the beetroot, make sure all the juice has been squeezed out before mixing it with the other ingredients. Combine vegetables and spoon mixture into open pitta pocket. Sprinkle with dill and pepper.

Carrot, Cheese, Apple and
Pecan Nut Pitta

FILLS ½ PITTA

¼ cup grated carrot
¼ cup grated low-fat grating
  cheese
¼ cup diced apple
2–3 pecan nuts, roughly chopped
black pepper to taste
½ small wholemeal pitta bread

Combine all ingredients. Mix well,
and spoon into open pitta pocket.

Chicken, Lettuce, Cucumber
and Spring Onion Pitta

FILLS ½ PITTA

¼ cup chopped cooked chicken
¼ cup shredded lettuce
2 tablespoons diced cucumber
1 tablespoon chopped spring onion
½ small wholemeal pitta bread

Make sure all the skin and fat have
been removed from the chicken
before cooking. Combine all
ingredients. Mix well, and spoon
into open pitta pocket.

Coleslaw Pitta

FILLS ½ PITTA

¾ cup coleslaw (see pages 45,
  47–8)
½ small wholemeal pitta bread

Spoon the coleslaw of your choice
into open pitta pocket.

Sardine Pitta

FILLS I PITTA

1 small wholemeal pitta bread
80 g sardines
squeeze of lemon juice
½ cup shredded lettuce
8 cucumber slices
¼ cup grated carrot
alfalfa sprouts for garnishing

Split the pitta bread into two circles. Drain sardines of their oil and squeeze lemon juice over them. Spread sardines over one side of pitta. Top with remaining ingredients, then other half of pitta.

Zucchini, Carrot and Mushroom Pitta

FILLS ½ PITTA

¼ cup grated zucchini
¼ cup grated carrot
¼ cup finely sliced mushroom
a little freshly chopped basil
a little freshly chopped parsley
a few sesame seeds
½ small wholemeal pitta bread

After grating the zucchini, make sure all the juice has been squeezed out before mixing it with the other ingredients. Combine all ingredients. Mix well, and spoon into open pitta pocket.

Indian Curry Dip

MAKES I CUP

1 cup non-fat or low-fat yoghurt
1 teaspoon curry powder
1 teaspoon ground cummin

Add a little yoghurt to the spices and blend well. Add remaining yoghurt and mix through. Cover and chill.

Minted Sambal Dip

4 spring onions
300 ml non-fat or low-fat yoghurt
1 teaspoon finely grated fresh
   ginger
1 tablespoon curry powder
6–8 tablespoons freshly chopped
   mint
1 clove garlic, crushed

Finely chop the spring onions and combine with all the remaining ingredients. Cover and chill well. The flavour will improve as the dip stands.

Pitta Crisps

small wholemeal pitta breads
a little onion powder or garlic
   powder
a little Parmesan cheese or tomato
   paste and sesame seeds

Preheat oven to 200°C.

Split pitta pocket circles in half and cut each half into 4 pieces. Sprinkle with a little onion powder or garlic powder and a little Parmesan cheese, or wipe with a little tomato paste and sprinkle with sesame seeds. Place on a non-stick baking sheet or straight on a baking tray and cook in preheated oven until browned. Cool and store in an airtight container.

For a tasty, crunchy snack, use for nibbling or dipping into your favourite dip combination.

Carrot, Currant and Parsley Sandwich

grated carrot
currants
finely chopped fresh parsley
unsweetened orange juice
lettuce
black pepper to taste
finely chopped spring onions
2 slices wholegrain, fat-free or
  low-fat bread

Marinate carrot, currants and parsley in orange juice for 1 hour. Drain well. Place lettuce on a slice of bread. Add the carrot filling, season with pepper, top with spring onions and more lettuce and another slice of bread.

Cottage Cheese and Banana Sandwich

low-fat cottage cheese
mashed banana
sultanas or chopped dates or figs
2 slices wholegrain, fat-free or
  low-fat bread

Combine ingredients between two slices of your favourite bread.

Curried Chicken and Celery Sandwich

lettuce
diced cooked chicken (all skin and
   fat removed before cooking),
   about 100–125 g per serve
finely diced celery
finely diced apple
Yoghurt Curry Dressing
   (see page 51)
2 slices wholegrain, fat-free or
   low-fat bread

Place lettuce on a slice of bread.
Combine chicken, celery, apple and
dressing in a bowl and toss well.
Spread over lettuce. Top with more
lettuce and another slice of bread.

Grated Vegetable Sandwich

lettuce
grated carrot
grated beetroot (juice squeezed
   out)
grated zucchini (juice squeezed
   out)
grated red salad onion
grated low-fat grating cheese
   (about 25 g per serve)
black pepper to taste
2 slices wholegrain, fat-free or
   low-fat bread

Place lettuce on a slice of bread.
Place grated vegetables and cheese
in a bowl and mix well. Spread
over lettuce, and season with
pepper. Top with lettuce and
another slice of bread.

Lettuce, Tomato, Onion and Sprouts Sandwich

lettuce
thickly sliced tomato
thinly sliced red salad onion
finely chopped fresh basil or chives
alfalfa sprouts
black pepper to taste
2 slices wholegrain, fat-free or
  low-fat bread

Place lettuce on a slice of bread. Top with tomato, onion, more tomato and more onion. Sprinkle with herbs. Add alfalfa sprouts, season with pepper and top with another slice of bread.

Salmon, Cucumber and Sprouts Sandwich

lettuce
sliced Salmon and Ricotta Terrine
  (see page 82)
sliced cucumber
thinly sliced red salad onion
  (optional)
alfalfa sprouts
2 slices wholegrain, fat-free or
  low-fat bread

Place lettuce on a slice of bread. Add a slice of terrine. Top with cucumber slices, onion slices and alfalfa sprouts, and another slice of bread.

Broccoli and Cauliflower Muffins

200 g broccoli florets
200 g cauliflower florets
2 cups oat bran
1 teaspoon grated Parmesan cheese
1 cup unbleached wholemeal flour
1 cup unbleached white flour
6 teaspoons baking powder
1 teaspoon ground nutmeg
1¼ cups low-fat evaporated skim milk
½ cup cold pressed grapeseed oil
¼ cup apple juice concentrate
4 egg whites

Preheat oven to 180°C.

Steam broccoli and cauliflower until just tender and plunge into cold water. Drain well. Place oat bran and cheese in a large bowl. Sift flours, baking powder and nutmeg over oat bran and cheese. Add broccoli and cauliflower and toss through the flour mixture to coat well.

Combine milk, oil and apple juice concentrate and stir into the flour and oat mixture. Be careful not to break up cauliflower and broccoli pieces.

Beat egg whites until stiff peaks form, and gently fold them through the mixture. Spoon into a lightly oiled and 'oat branned' muffin tray. Bake for 25–30 minutes.

Remove muffins from the tray immediately and place on a wire rack to cool. Cover with a tea towel.

Cauliflower and Cheese Oat Bran Muffins

MAKES 12 LARGE MUFFINS

2 cups oat bran
2 cups unbleached white flour
6 teaspoons baking powder
1 teaspoon ground nutmeg
100 g low-fat grating cheese
500 g very small cauliflower florets
½ cup cold pressed grapeseed oil
1½ cups low-fat milk or low-fat soymilk
3 egg whites

Preheat oven to 180°C.

Place oat bran in a large bowl. Sift flour, baking powder and nutmeg over the oat bran. Grate cheese and distribute it through the flour mixture with your hands. Steam cauliflower until just tender. Plunge into cold water to cool. Drain well. Add cauliflower florets to the flour and oat mixture and coat well with flour.

Combine oil and milk and stir through the flour and cauliflower mixture. Be careful not to break up the cauliflower pieces.

Beat egg whites until stiff peaks form and gently fold them through the muffin mixture. Spoon into lightly oiled muffin tray. The mixture will come up over the top of the tray. Bake for 25–30 minutes.

Remove muffins from the tray immediately and place on a wire rack to cool. Cover with a tea towel.

Opposite
Artichoke and Leek Pizza Slice (see page 41) with Grapefruit and Orange Juice (see page 5).

Artichoke and Leek Pizza Slice

1 quantity Scone Dough
(see Asparagus and Cheese Pizza
Wheel, page 42)
¾ cup Pizza Sauce (see below)
1 × 400 g can artichoke hearts,
well drained
1 leek, washed, sliced, steamed and
well drained
100 g low-fat grating cheese

PIZZA SAUCE
3 medium-sized onions, diced
2 cloves garlic, crushed
2 × 400 g cans salt-free tomatoes,
puréed
1 cup tomato paste
½ teaspoon dried basil
1 teaspoon dried oregano

Preheat oven to 220°C.

Roll out scone dough into a circle
or a rectangle.

To make the pizza sauce, cook
onion and garlic in a little water
until soft. Add remaining ingredients
and boil for 5 minutes. Set aside to
cool. (This recipe makes about
5 cups of sauce so you will not need
it all for the pizza. The sauce stores
well in an airtight jar in the
refrigerator and can also be frozen.)

Spread the pizza sauce over the
base. Slice artichoke hearts and
place on top of the pizza with the
sliced leek. Grate cheese and
sprinkle on top of the artichoke and
leek. Bake the pizza in the
preheated oven for 20 minutes.

Serve with soup or a salad.

Opposite
Peachy Beef Strips (see page 70).

Asparagus and Cheese Pizza Wheel

SCONE DOUGH

1½ cups unbleached white flour
½ cup oat bran
3 teaspoons baking powder
1 tablespoon lemon juice
1 tablespoon non-fat or low-fat yoghurt
½ cup low-fat milk or low-fat soymilk

FILLING

1 × 340 g can asparagus spears, well drained and mashed
100 g low-fat grating cheese
a little cayenne pepper

Preheat oven to 200°C.

Sift flour, oat bran and baking powder into a bowl. Combine lemon juice and yoghurt and add to the flour mixture. Rub in with your fingers. Add milk and work into a firm dough. Place on a lightly floured bench and knead well. Roll out to a rectangular shape, approximately 26 × 22 cm. Use a sharp knife to cut away any uneven edges.

Spread asparagus evenly over the dough. Grate cheese and sprinkle half of it over the asparagus. Carefully roll up to make a long log.

Using a very sharp knife, cut the log into 8 pieces. Line a baking tray with non-stick baking paper and place circles flat on it, starting at the centre and working outwards so that the circles as a whole form a circular shape. The circles should almost touch. Sprinkle with remaining cheese and a little cayenne pepper. Cook in preheated oven for 20 minutes or until well browned.

Serve with soup or a salad.

Eggplant and Potato Pizza

SERVES 4–6

1 quantity Scone Dough
  (see page 42)
¾ cup Pizza Sauce (see page 41)
1 teaspoon light olive oil
1 small eggplant, cut into thin
  rounds
1 large potato, peeled and cut into
  thin rounds
100 g low-fat grating cheese

Preheat oven to 180°C.

Make up scone dough and pizza
sauce.

Lightly oil a baking tray with the
oil. Lay eggplant rounds on the
tray. Bake in oven until eggplant
changes colour and softens.
Remove from oven and allow to
cool.

Lightly steam potato slices until just
tender, but still firm. Drain and
cool.

Increase oven temperature to
220°C. Roll out scone dough to
required shape. Spread with pizza
sauce. Top with overlapping
eggplant and potato rounds. Grate
cheese, sprinkle on top of the
vegetables, and bake for 20 minutes.

Serve with a salad.

Sardine, Mushroom and Onion Oat Bran Pizza

SERVES 6–8

1 quantity Basic Oat Bran Bread
  dough (see page 114)
½ cup low-fat grating cheese
  (optional)
1 cup Pizza Sauce (see page 41)
2 × 125 g cans sardines
juice of 1 lemon
1 onion

200 g thinly sliced mushroom
½ cup finely chopped fresh chives
50–100 g low-fat grating cheese
black pepper to taste

The dough makes two pizza bases –
or one base and one small loaf of
bread. You can store half the dough

in an airtight plastic bag in the refrigerator and use the following day for a pizza base or a small bread loaf. Keeping it in the refrigerator will stop the yeast from working. Once it comes back to room temperature, the yeast will begin to work. For a very crisp pizza base (optional), omit the calcium ascorbate in the Basic Oat Bran Bread recipe, and add ½ cup of low-fat grating cheese.

Preheat oven to 220°C.

Following the Basic Oat Bran Bread recipe, place flour, oat bran, yeast and calcium ascorbate (if using) in a large mixing bowl. Mix to combine ingredients. Add low-fat cheese (if using), oil, and apple juice concentrate. Pour in the very warm water and use a knife to scrape flour away from the sides of the bowl.

Mix in a food mixer (using bread dough hook) on low speed for approximately 6–7 minutes. Alternatively, mix as much as possible with the knife, then turn the dough out onto a floured bench (use only unbleached white flour) and begin kneading. The longer you knead, the better the end result will be.

If mixing in a food mixer, turn dough out onto a floured bench and knead to make a good firm shape. The bread will be firm but sticky when it leaves the bowl.

Roll out half the dough into pizza tray shape. (If using the rest of the dough for a loaf, follow the basic breadmaking instructions on page 113.) Spread the pizza sauce over the base.

Drain oil from sardines and squeeze lemon juice over them. Break up sardines and distribute over the pizza sauce. Slice onion into rings and spread over top of the sardines. Add mushroom and chives, grate cheese and sprinkle with a little pepper on top. Cook in a very hot oven for approximately 20 minutes.

Salmon and Cottage Cheese Pizza SERVES 4

1 quantity Scone Dough
(see page 42)
1 × 440 g can red salmon, well
drained
1 medium zucchini, grated (juice
squeezed out)
½ cup low-fat cottage cheese
1 tablespoon grated horseradish
1 tablespoon finely chopped fresh
chives
100 g low-fat grating cheese

Preheat oven to 220°C.

Roll dough out to a round or
rectangular shape. Place on a flat
baking tray.

Mix together salmon, zucchini,
cottage cheese, horseradish and
chives. Spread over the dough.
Grate cheese and sprinkle over the
top.

Bake in preheated oven for
15–20 minutes or until base looks
crisp and top is lightly browned.

Avocado Coleslaw SERVES 1 OR 2–3 AS SIDE SALAD

100 g thinly sliced cabbage
100 g avocado, cut into bite-sized
squares
50 g grated carrot
50 g grated cucumber, seeds
removed
50 g diced green capsicum

Combine all ingredients with your
favourite dressing. Toss gently to
avoid squashing the avocado.

Broccoli, Cauliflower, Tomato and Pine Nut Salad

SERVES 2–3

100 g broccoli florets
100 g cauliflower florets
100 g cherry tomatoes, halved
2 tablespoons pine nuts
fresh basil leaves

Blanch broccoli and cauliflower in boiling water, plunge into cold water, and drain well. Combine all ingredients and toss in your favourite dressing.

Carrot, Parsley, Broccoli and Currant Salad

SERVES 1 OR 2–3 AS SIDE SALAD

1 cup finely chopped fresh parsley
1 cup broccoli florets
1 cup grated carrot
2 tablespoons currants

(This salad relies on very fresh parsley for a good flavour.) Blanch broccoli florets in boiling water, plunge in cold water, and drain well. Combine all ingredients.

You will not require dressing as the moisture of the carrot and parsley and their combined flavours are just perfect by themselves.

Corn Coleslaw

SERVES 1 OR 2–3 AS SIDE SALAD

100 g thinly sliced cabbage
100 g corn kernels, cooked
50 g grated carrot
2 spring onions, thinly sliced
50 g thinly sliced celery
50 g diced red and green capsicum

Combine all ingredients. Toss in your favourite dressing. Stand for 1 hour to develop the flavours.

Orange Coleslaw

SERVES 1 OR 2–3 AS SIDE SALAD

100 g thinly sliced cabbage
1½ oranges
50 g sliced celery
50 g grated carrot
1 spring onion, thinly sliced
2 tablespoons freshly chopped
   herbs

Peel oranges, cut them into quarters and thinly slice. Combine all ingredients (the herbs should preferably be thyme and marjoram). Toss in your favourite dressing. Stand for 1 hour before serving to allow the flavours to develop.

Red and Green Coleslaw

SERVES 4

200 g winter (purple) cabbage, shredded
100 g green cabbage or lettuce, shredded
100 g red capsicums
50 g green capsicums
10 snowpeas
2 spring onions
black pepper to taste

Combine shredded cabbage, and lettuce (if using). Cut capsicums and snowpeas into julienne strips. Chop spring onion, and then toss all ingredients with a dressing of your choice.

You can substitute kohlrabi in any coleslaw recipe where a cabbage is required. Use a little or a lot of it, depending on your requirements.

Zucchini, Carrot and Sesame Seed Salad

SERVES 1 OR 2–3 AS SIDE SALAD

100 g carrots
100 g zucchini
2 tablespoons finely chopped fresh thyme
2 teaspoons sesame seeds

Prepare julienne strips of carrot and zucchini. Place in a bowl and add thyme and sesame seeds.

Carrot combines well with zucchini, and this salad looks great if the ingredients are cut into very fine, even julienne lengths. Of course it helps if you have a kitchen utensil that will do this job for you, but if not persevere because the end result is worth it.

French Dressing

1 cup light cold pressed olive oil
4 tablespoons lemon juice
1 tablespoon wholegrain mustard
a little grated lemon rind
a little grated orange rind
2 cloves garlic, crushed (optional)

Place all ingredients in a screw-top jar and shake well. Store in refrigerator. The lemon and orange rind infuses a subtle flavour as the dressing stands over a period of time. Shake well before use, and use moderately as olive oil contains valuable monounsaturated fats.

Garlic Vinaigrette

¾ cup unsweetened apple juice
½ cup wine vinegar
2 tablespoons lemon juice
2 teaspoons grated lemon rind
4 small cloves garlic, crushed

Combine all ingredients in a screw-top jar and keep in refrigerator. Shake every now and then, and particularly before use.

Hazelnut or Walnut Dressing

½ cup light cold pressed olive oil
2 tablespoons lemon juice
1 tablespoon finely chopped
  hazelnuts or walnuts

Mix ingredients together. Leave to stand for 7 days before using. Shake well before use, and use moderately as olive oil contains valuable monounsaturated fats. Hazelnuts and walnuts contain some polyunsaturated fats.

Herb Vinaigrette

¾ cup unsweetened apple or pear
or orange juice
½ cup wine vinegar
1 tablespoon apple juice
concentrate
6 tablespoons freshly chopped

herbs (e.g. thyme, oregano, basil,
marjoram, chives, parsley)

Combine all ingredients in a
screw-top jar and keep in
refrigerator. Shake well before use.

Spicy Tomato Dressing

1 cup tomato juice
1 cup freshly squeezed orange juice
grated rind of 1 orange
¼ cup vinegar
2 small cloves garlic, crushed
½ teaspoon dried oregano
½ teaspoon dried basil
a little cayenne pepper
3 teaspoons arrowroot
1 tablespoon water

Combine all ingredients, except
arrowroot and water, in a saucepan
and slowly bring to the boil. Mix
arrowroot with water and add to
the pan. Stir as dressing thickens.
Simmer for 2 minutes, then leave to
cool. Store in refrigerator.

Tahini Dressing

½ cup tahini (use one that is firm,
without oil sitting on top)
2 tablespoons lemon juice
1 tablespoon horseradish paste
a little crushed garlic (optional)

Combine all ingredients and thin to
the desired consistency with water
in a blender. Use moderately as
tahini is made from sesame seeds,
which contain polyunsaturated fats.

Yoghurt Curry Dressing

½ cup non-fat or low-fat yoghurt
1 teaspoon curry powder
1 teaspoon tomato paste
1 tablespoon unsweetened orange
  juice

Mix all ingredients together
thoroughly in a screw-top jar and
keep refrigerated.

Soymilk Mayonnaise

¾ cup low-fat soymilk
¼ cup apple juice concentrate
2 teaspoons Dijon mustard
½ cup wine vinegar

Place all ingredients in a screw-top
jar and shake well. Store in
refrigerator. Shake well before each
use.

VARIATION
- For a dill-flavoured mayonnaise,
  add 2 teaspoons of finely
  chopped fresh dill.

Baked Potato Bolognese

unpeeled potatoes, washed
Bolognese Sauce (see page 71)
low-fat cottage cheese

Preheat oven to 200°C.

Place the desired number of potatoes on the oven rack and bake until the outside is crunchy and the centre is soft – about 1 hour.

Remove potatoes from the oven, make some cuts in the top and fill with bolognese sauce (an ideal way to use up the left-over sauce from spaghetti) and top with cottage cheese. Serve with a salad.

Baked Potatoes with Cheese and Capsicum

unpeeled potatoes, washed
low-fat cottage cheese
grated low-fat grating cheese
diced red and green capsicum

Preheat oven to 200°C.

Place the desired number of potatoes in the oven and bake for about 1 hour.

Remove potatoes from the oven, cut open and fill with a mixture of the cheeses and capsicum. Serve with a salad.

Beans Spud

unpeeled potatoes, washed
low-fat cottage cheese
any combination of beans
  (e.g. kidney beans, butter beans,
  garbanzo beans, lima beans),
  cooked
grated low-fat grating cheese

Preheat oven to 200°C.

Place potatoes in the oven and bake until cooked – about 1 hour.

Combine cottage cheese with cooked beans. Remove potatoes from the oven, open at the top and fill with the cheese and bean mixture. Top with grated cheese and serve with a salad.

Mushroom Potatoes

unpeeled potatoes, washed
Mushroom Sauce (see page 25)

Preheat oven to 200°C.

Place the desired number of potatoes on the oven rack and bake until the outside is crunchy and the centre is soft – about 1 hour.

Remove potatoes from the oven, open at the top and fill with mushroom sauce. Serve with a salad.

Salmon Dip Potatoes

unpeeled potatoes, washed
alfalfa sprouts

SALMON DIP
2 cups well-drained salmon
225 g low-fat cottage cheese
3 tablespoons tomato paste
I tablespoon lemon juice
black pepper to taste
3 shallots, finely chopped (optional)

Preheat oven to 200°C.

Place potatoes in the oven and bake until cooked – about 1 hour.

Combine all ingredients for the dip, except shallots, in a food processor, and blend until smooth. Fold in shallots.

Remove potatoes from the oven, open at the top and fill with salmon dip. Top with alfalfa sprouts and serve. (This dip is also good served with vegetable crudités, in sandwiches, or as a filling for lettuce cups with a lot of grated vegetables.)

Low
Cholesterol
Soups

Chicken Vegetable Soup

2 cups Chicken Stock (see below)
1 onion, chopped
1 teaspoon crushed garlic
500 g carrots
500 g zucchini
500 g celery, washed
500 g leeks, washed
200 g parsnips
200 g swedes
200 g turnips
2 chicken drumsticks (all skin and
    fat removed before cooking)
2 cups salt-free tomato juice
1 teaspoon dried basil
1 teaspoon dried oregano
black pepper to taste

CHICKEN STOCK
1 chicken or chicken carcass
1 stick celery, roughly chopped
1 carrot, roughly chopped
1 onion, roughly chopped
a little freshly chopped parsley
6 black peppercorns

First make the chicken stock. Place chicken or chicken carcass in a large pot with celery, carrot, onion, parsley and peppercorns. Cover with water and simmer for 2 hours. Strain off the stock, discarding the bones, meat and vegetables. Chill the stock to congeal any fat, and remove this before using. (Chicken stock stores well in the freezer.)

To make the vegetable soup, cook onion and garlic in a large saucepan with a little chicken stock, until the onion softens.

Chop all remaining vegetables finely, and add to the pan with the chicken stock and all other ingredients. Cook until vegetables are soft and chicken is tender – about 30–40 minutes.

Remove chicken from the bones, return the meat to the soup and discard the bones.

Hearty Lamb Shank
Vegetable Soup

SERVES 4–6

1 onion, chopped
1 teaspoon crushed garlic
2 cups water
500 g carrots
500 g zucchini
500 g celery, washed
500 g leeks, washed
200 g parsnips
200 g swedes
200 g turnips
2 lamb shanks
2 cups salt-free tomato juice
1 teaspoon dried mixed herbs
black pepper to taste
½ cup cooked red kidney beans

In a large pot cook onion and garlic in a little of the water until onion is soft. Chop all remaining vegetables and add to the pot along with lamb shanks, tomato juice, herbs, seasoning and the rest of the water. Cook for 1–1½ hours, until vegetables are soft and lamb is tender. Allow to cool.

When cold (chill in the refrigerator if necessary) remove all fat. Remove all meat from lamb shanks, return meat to soup and discard the bones. Finally add kidney beans and reheat to serve.

Peppery Pumpkin Bean Soup

SERVES 4–6

1 large onion, diced
1 teaspoon crushed garlic
1 tablespoon Vecon (natural
  vegetable stock available at health
  food stores)
4½ cups water
700 g pumpkin, peeled and
  chopped
¼ teaspoon black pepper
1 × 750 g can 4 Bean Mix
a handful of finely chopped fresh
  chives or a little finely chopped
  fresh thyme

In a large saucepan cook onion and garlic with Vecon and ½ cup of the water until onion has softened. Add remaining water, pumpkin and pepper. Cook until pumpkin is soft and then place the contents of the pan in a blender and purée. Return to the pan.

Rinse beans under running water to wash off excess salt and sugar. Add beans and fresh herbs to the soup. Heat through and serve.

Asparagus and Spinach Broth

SERVES 2

2 cups Vegetable Broth (see page
  63)
100 g fresh asparagus spears
½ small onion, finely chopped
100 g fresh spinach, torn into small
  pieces
black pepper to taste

Make up broth according to the recipe. Cook asparagus and onion in the vegetable broth over low heat until they are nearly tender. Add spinach and cook until spinach has just changed to a bright green colour. Season to taste with black pepper.

Avocado Soup

1 avocado (about 150 g flesh)
200 g celery
300 g carrots
squeeze of lemon juice
black pepper to taste
a handful of finely chopped fresh
   chives (optional)

(This is a raw chilled soup.) Purée avocado and juice the celery and carrots. Add the juice to the avocado and continue to purée for a thick, creamy, smooth-textured soup. Season to taste with lemon juice and black pepper. Garnish with chopped chives and serve chilled.

You can extend this soup by thinning it with Vegetable Broth (see page 63).

Broccoli and Cauliflower Broth

1 litre Vegetable Broth
   (see page 63)
2 cloves garlic, crushed
2 cups thinly sliced broccoli
2 cups thinly sliced cauliflower
a little freshly chopped marjoram
a little freshly chopped thyme

Make up broth and bring it to a gentle simmer. Add garlic, broccoli and cauliflower. Cover and cook until vegetables are just tender.

Serve garnished with freshly chopped herbs.

Carrot and Herb Soup

½ litre carrot juice, chilled
½ cup finely chopped fresh herbs
  (e.g. parsley, chives, thyme,
  oregano, marjoram, basil)
¼ cup thinly sliced celery

(This is a raw chilled soup.)
Combine all ingredients and serve.

Carrot, Tomato and Basil Soup

½ litre carrot juice, chilled
½ litre tomato juice, chilled
lots of black pepper
¼–½ cup finely chopped fresh basil
a little celery powder (optional)

(This is a raw chilled soup.)
Combine all ingredients, except
celery powder. Mix well and serve.
If tomatoes are too acidic, you
could add a little celery powder to
taste.

Carrot and Walnut Soup

¼ cup walnuts
½ litre Vegetable Broth
  (see page 63)
½ litre carrot juice
a little ground nutmeg

(This is a raw chilled soup.) Make
sure walnuts are fresh or they will
give a bitter taste.

Make up broth. Place walnuts in a
food processor and process until
powdery. Add carrot juice, then
broth. Serve in individual bowls
and garnish with a sprinkle of
nutmeg.

Cucumber, Carrot and Ginger Broth

1 litre Vegetable Broth
  (see page 63)
50 g peeled ginger
300 g peeled cucumber
300 g peeled carrots
¼ cup finely chopped fresh parsley

Make up broth. Cut ginger, cucumber and carrots into very fine, even julienne lengths. In a separate saucepan, cook ginger in a little broth until soft. Add all remaining ingredients except parsley. Cover and simmer until carrot and cucumber are just soft. Add parsley and serve.

Gazpacho

SERVES 4–6

1 kg ripe tomatoes
200 g carrots
150 g cucumber
2 large cloves garlic, crushed
2 tablespoons finely chopped fresh
  herbs (e.g. basil, oregano, thyme)
lots of black pepper

(This is a raw chilled soup.) Juice tomatoes, carrots and cucumber. Add remaining ingredients and stir through. Chill and stir occasionally to develop the flavours.

Melon Soup

200 g cantaloup, peeled and seeded
200 g honeydew melon, peeled and
  seeded
2–3 cm piece fresh ginger, peeled
a little fresh mint

(This is a raw chilled soup.) Juice melons and ginger. Chop fresh mint finely and stir through. Serve well chilled.

Potato Soup

1½ litres Vegetable Broth
  (see page 63)
2 onions, chopped
2 cloves garlic, crushed
1 teaspoon ground cummin
½ teaspoon ground ginger
¼ teaspoon turmeric
¼ teaspoon ground nutmeg
¼ teaspoon dry mustard
1 kg potatoes, peeled and chopped
200 g chopped celery

Make up broth. In a separate pan, cook onion and garlic in a little broth to soften, then add spices and cook for a few minutes. Add remaining ingredients and simmer until potatoes are soft. Purée, then return to the pan to reheat.

Pumpkin and Coriander Soup

SERVES 4

4 cups water or Vegetable Broth
  (see page 63)
2 medium-sized onions, chopped
1 tablespoon fresh ginger, peeled
  and chopped
1 teaspoon turmeric
2 teaspoons coriander powder
500 g pumpkin, peeled and
  chopped

Make up broth (if using).

Place onion and ginger in a
saucepan. Cover and cook on a
gentle heat until onion is soft and
almost transparent (if onion and
ginger are sticking you have got the
cooking temperature too high –
adding just a little water will ease
the foodstuffs off the bottom of the
saucepan).

Add spices and cook for a further
minute. Add pumpkin and water or
broth and cook until pumpkin is
tender. Purée, then return to the
stove to reheat.

Vegetable Broth

MAKES 3 LITRES

4½ litres water
½ bunch celery (including green
  leaves), roughly chopped
2 large brown onions
2 large carrots, roughly chopped
a generous handful parsley
1 tablespoon pink peppercorns

Put water and celery in a saucepan.
Top and tail onions and wash any
dirt off the skins. Cut onions in half
and add (skin intact) to the pot
with remaining ingredients. Bring
to the boil. Turn down and simmer
for 2½–3 hours. Strain through a
fine sieve.

This is a very clear liquid full of
goodness and flavour that is
excellent served as a clear broth
with finely chopped fresh herbs.
Alternatively, grate some vegetables
and add to the stock, and bring to
the boil so that the vegetables are
just cooked. The broth can also be
used as a vegetable stock to enhance
the flavour of other soups, or it can
be used as the base of other soups.

Low
Cholesterol
Main
Meals

Caraway Beef

1 teaspoon olive oil
1 onion, diced
1 teaspoon caraway seeds
600 g lean minced beef
2 × 285 g cans white champignons
2 cups low-fat milk or low-fat
  soymilk
¼ cup cornflour
black pepper to taste

Put oil in a large saucepan and cook onion and caraway seeds over gentle heat until soft. Add meat. Use a wooden spoon to break up the meat as it cooks. Cook for approximately 10 minutes or until all the meat has changed colour. Add champignons and cover. Cook for a further 20 minutes on very low heat. Combine the soymilk and cornflour to make a paste and add to the meat. Stir until sauce thickens. Add black pepper to taste.

Serve with brown rice, or noodles and a salad.

Family Meatloaf

1 onion, finely chopped
1 teaspoon finely diced garlic
100 g finely sliced mushroom
500 g lean minced beef
100 g grated zucchini (juice
  squeezed out)
100 g grated carrot
½ cup frozen peas
2 Granny Smith apples, peeled and
  grated (juice squeezed out)
1 egg white
1 cup rolled oats
1 teaspoon basil flakes
½ teaspoon dried oregano
½ teaspoon ground cummin or
  dried thyme
½ cup finely chopped fresh parsley
black pepper to taste

TOPPING
3 tablespoons tomato paste
200 g low-fat grating cheese
½ cup rolled oats

Preheat oven to 180°C.

In a saucepan cook onion, garlic and mushroom together until just soft (you may need to add a teaspoon of water to prevent sticking).

Place all remaining meatloaf ingredients in a large bowl. Add cooked ingredients from the pan and mix well using your hands. Press mixture firmly into a lightly oiled meatloaf dish.

Spoon tomato paste over meatloaf. Grate cheese, combine with oats, and sprinkle over the meatloaf. Cover dish and cook in a water bath in preheated oven for approximately 1 hour. Remove cover and cook a further 10 minutes to brown the top.

Beef and Vegetable Casserole

2 tablespoons tomato paste
2 tablespoons low-salt soy sauce
1 tablespoon apple juice
  concentrate
½ teaspoon ground cinnamon
1 teaspoon ground nutmeg
600 g blade steak (all fat and sinew
  removed), cut into bite-sized
  chunks
2 teaspoons crushed garlic
2 onions, quartered and sliced
250 g carrots, cut into rounds
250 g parsnips, cut into rounds
250 g swedes, cut into chunks
250 g zucchini, cut into rounds
1 red capsicum, cut into chunks
¾ cup red wine
1 cup water
2–4 tablespoons cornflour
1 cup frozen peas

Mix together tomato paste, soy sauce, apple juice concentrate, cinnamon and nutmeg, and marinate steak in this marinade for at least 1 hour before cooking. Turn meat frequently.

When ready to cook, preheat oven to 200°C. Drain meat. Heat wok until very hot and cook meat in 3 batches, turning quickly to brown on both sides. Remove meat to a large casserole dish and clean wok.

Cook garlic, onion, carrot, parsnip, swede, zucchini and capsicum in a little water in the wok until they just begin to soften. Remove from the stove and place vegetables in the dish with the meat. Add wine and ¼ cup of the water. Cover and cook in preheated oven for 1½–2 hours, or until meat is tender.

Combine cornflour with ¾ cup of water and add to the casserole. Stir to thicken. Add peas. Cook a further 15 minutes.

Serve with pappadams.

Gravy Beef Ramekins

1 onion, diced
1 carrot, grated
1 stick celery, chopped
400 g gravy beef (all fat and sinew removed)
4 cups water
½ cup frozen peas
¾ cup corn kernels, cooked
black pepper to taste
2–3 tablespoons cornflour
1 tablespoon extra water
¼ cup finely chopped fresh chives
6 cups cooked mashed potato

Simmer onion, carrot, celery and gravy beef in the 4 cups of water for approximately 3 hours or until gravy beef is tender. Mix in a blender or food processor to break up meat, but do not purée to a pulp. Add peas, corn and pepper.

Mix cornflour with the 1 tablespoon of extra water to make a paste. Stir through the meat mixture and cook until thickened. Add chives.

Preheat oven to 200°C.

Spoon mixture into 4 large individual ramekins. Top with mashed potato. Cook in preheated oven until potato has browned and mixture is bubbling.

Serve with a salad.

Peachy Beef Strips

2 onions, quartered and sliced
1 teaspoon crushed garlic
1 teaspoon olive oil
350–400 g beef fillet (all fat and
   sinew removed), cut into thin
   strips
1 teaspoon ground cummin
1 teaspoon curry powder
½ teaspoon ground cinnamon
1 cup unsweetened peach juice
1 cup water
1 cup unsweetened peach pieces
2 zucchini, cut into diagonal slices
   and lightly steamed

In a wok or non-stick pan cook the onion and garlic in oil until onion just begins to turn in colour. Add beef strips and toss until all the meat has browned. Add spices and continue cooking for about 2 minutes. Add peach juice and water. Cover and cook until meat is tender and sauce has reduced and thickened. Add peach pieces and zucchini. Heat through before serving.

Serve with wholemeal noodles or brown rice.

Spaghetti Bolognese

1 × 500 g packet semolina
spaghetti

BOLOGNESE SAUCE
2 onions, chopped
1 teaspoon crushed garlic
700 g lean minced beef
1 teaspoon dried basil
1 teaspoon dried oregano
½ teaspoon dried thyme
1 cup rolled oats
1 cup red wine
2 × 400 g cans whole tomatoes in
natural juice, salt-free
1 × 140 g tub tomato paste

To make bolognese sauce, place
onion and garlic in a large non-stick
pan and cook gently until soft. Add
meat a little at a time. Use a
wooden spoon to break up meat as
it browns. Turn meat frequently
until all meat has browned (do not
have the heat up too high or the
meat and onions will burn rather
than brown).

Add herbs and rolled oats. Cook for
2 minutes, stirring frequently. Add
wine. Chop tomatoes and add to
the pan with the juice and tomato
paste. Bring to the boil. Turn heat
down to a simmer. Stir frequently
to avoid sticking and cook,
uncovered, for 20–30 minutes, or
until sauce is thick and a rich red
colour.

To cook spaghetti, follow
instructions on packet. Serve
spaghetti in bowls topped with
sauce.

**SERVING SUGGESTIONS (FOR
LEFT-OVER BOLOGNESE SAUCE)**
- Serve on hot toast as a
  lunchtime snack.
- Serve in hot baked potatoes.
- Scoop out the inside of suitable
  vegetables (for example, eggplant,
  baby pumpkins, zucchini) and
  steam or bake the vegetables
  until just tender. Fill the
  vegetables with sauce and top
  with some grated low-fat grating
  cheese. Return vegetables to the
  oven and bake until sauce has
  heated through and cheese is
  brown. Serve with a salad.
- Use as a topping for pizza.
- Use sauce as a filling for
  wholemeal lasagne.

Chicken and Eggplant Lasagne Slice SERVES 6

2 medium-sized onions, diced
2 teaspoons olive oil or
  2 tablespoons water
600 g chicken meat (all skin and fat
  removed), cut into cubes
3 cups low-fat milk or low-fat
  soymilk
1 teaspoon dried dill
1 teaspoon dried basil
½ cup cornflour
200 g eggplant, cut into cubes
200 g red capsicums, chopped
200 g broccoli florets, sliced
200 g zucchini, sliced
1 × 200 g packet wholemeal
  lasagne pasta

CHEESE SAUCE
2 tablespoons cornflour
1 cup low-fat milk or low-fat
  soymilk
black pepper to taste
100 g low-fat grating cheese, grated

TOPPING
2 tablespoons oat bran
1 tablespoon grated Parmesan
  cheese

In a large saucepan cook onions over gentle heat in half of the oil or water. Add chicken. Toss frequently and cook for 10 minutes with the lid on. Add 2½ cups of the milk or soymilk, and the herbs. Mix together cornflour and remaining milk. Stir through chicken and milk, and stir until sauce thickens.

While chicken is cooking, in another saucepan cook the eggplant with the remaining oil or water. (I prefer oil here, because it gives the vegetables a roasted flavour, especially the eggplant.) When eggplant has softened, add other vegetables. Toss frequently and cook with lid on until all vegetables are tender. Add vegetables to the chicken in the saucepan.

To make cheese sauce, blend the cornflour with a little of the milk, and return to remaining milk. Add black pepper. Cook and stir sauce until it thickens. Turn off heat and add grated cheese.

Preheat oven to 180°C and assemble lasagne. Put a layer of pasta over base of lasagne dish. Top with chicken and vegetable mixture, another layer of pasta, another layer of chicken and vegetable mixture and cover with pasta. Spoon over the cheese sauce and sprinkle with the topping of combined oat bran and cheese.

Cook in preheated oven for approximately 30 minutes.

Chicken Fillet with Apple and Prunes in Lemon Sauce

SERVES 4

4 × 125 g chicken fillets (all fat and skin removed)
2 cups Chicken Stock (see page 56)
1 cup unsweetened orange juice
¼ cup cornflour
1 tablespoon lemon juice
grated rind of 1 lemon
1 tablespoon apple juice concentrate
1 teaspoon finely chopped fresh parsley
2 cooking apples, peeled and cored
12 moist prunes
1 cup water

Cook chicken fillets in 1 cup of chicken stock until they are just tender. Remove chicken. Mix a little of the orange juice with the cornflour to make a paste and stir into the stock in the pan. Add rest of the stock, lemon juice and rind, apple juice concentrate and parsley. Bring to the boil. Simmer until sauce thickens, then return chicken to the pan.

Cut each apple into 6 rings and cook with the prunes in water until apple rings are just tender but still holding their shape. Drain well.

Serve 1 chicken breast, 3 apple slices and 3 prunes per person and spoon the lemon sauce from the pan over the top.

Chicken, Leek and Artichoke Casserole

SERVES 6

1 × 1.4 kg chicken (all skin and fat removed)
2 teaspoons crushed garlic
1 large leek, cut into rounds
1 large carrot, cut into thin rounds
10 large mushrooms
1 tablespoon low-salt soy sauce
1 teaspoon light olive oil
1 cup dry white wine
¼ teaspoon dried rosemary
2 tablespoons cornflour
1 cup low-fat evaporated low-fat milk or low-fat soymilk
1 × 400 g can artichoke hearts, drained

Cut chicken into large pieces. Wipe garlic over the base of a non-stick pan. Heat the pan and brown the chicken pieces on both sides. Do not have pan too hot. Remove chicken pieces and place in a casserole dish.

Cook leek and carrot in a little water until carrot has softened slightly. Drain and add to the casserole.

Place mushrooms, soy sauce and oil in the pan. Cover and cook until mushrooms are soft. Check frequently to see that the mushrooms are not sticking to the pan. (If they are, turn the heat down.) Add cooked mushrooms to the casserole. Pour in wine and add rosemary. Cover and cook for 40–45 minutes. Remove from heat.

Combine cornflour and a little of the milk to make a paste. Add this to the remaining milk and stir through the casserole until sauce thickens. Continue cooking for another 15–20 minutes. Rinse artichoke hearts thoroughly in cold water to remove any salt. Cut them in half and add to the casserole. Leave the casserole standing, covered, for 5 minutes before serving, to allow the artichokes to heat through.

Serve with brown rice or salad.

Chicken Roll with Mustard Sauce

600 g chicken fillets (all skin and fat removed), minced
1 teaspoon finely chopped fresh ginger
1 teaspoon Dijon mustard
¼ cup tomato paste
¾ cup rolled oats
100 g broccoli florets, cut in half
1 long strip carrot (about 50 g)

MUSTARD SAUCE
1 cup unsweetened orange juice
½ cup dry sherry
2 teaspoons wholegrain mustard
2 tablespoons apple juice concentrate
2 tablespoons cornflour
3 tablespoons water or cooking liquid from chicken

Combine minced chicken, ginger, Dijon mustard, tomato paste and rolled oats in a bowl and mix well.

Steam broccoli and carrot until just tender. Take half the chicken mixture and flatten it out on the bench in a log shape. Top with broccoli and carrot running down the centre of the log. Top with remaining chicken. Press the ends and sides firmly together.

Place the chicken log in a frying pan or large shallow saucepan and add enough water to come halfway up the side of the chicken. Bring to the boil and simmer for 15 minutes. Turn chicken carefully and simmer for a further 15 minutes. Remove from water. Stand 5 minutes before slicing into 12 rounds. Serve with mustard sauce.

To make sauce, mix all ingredients together thoroughly and bring to the boil. Simmer and stir until sauce thickens. Pour sauce over the chicken roll just before serving. Accompany with steamed vegetables.

Fish in Dill Sauce

1 small onion
2 fillets sea perch
½ cup dry white wine
1 cup low-fat milk or low-fat
  soymilk
2 tablespoons cornflour
2 tablespoons freshly chopped dill
slices of lemon and fresh sprigs of
  dill for garnishing

Dice onion finely. Place onion, fish and white wine in a small pan. Cook gently until fish turns white and is cooked on both sides. Use a slotted spoon to remove fish. Keep warm.

Combine milk and cornflour to make a paste. Stir this through the pan juices and bring to the boil; stirring continuously until sauce thickens.

Return fish to the sauce. Sprinkle with chopped dill and heat through. Garnish with lemon slices and dill sprigs and serve immediately.

Fish Parcels with Lemon and Thyme SERVES 2

1 lemon, thinly sliced
2 fish fillets
¼–½ cup dry white wine
freshly chopped thyme

Cut out two large square pieces of foil. Place 2 slices of lemon on each piece of foil. Place a fillet of fish on top. Add more lemon. Pour wine over the fish and sprinkle them liberally with freshly chopped thyme.

Fold up foil to completely seal. Either cook on a hot barbecue or steam in water. On the barbecue the fish will take about 5–10 minutes to cook, depending on their size and the heat. If steaming, put 2 centimetres of water in the base of a pan. Put foil parcels in water, cover pan and leave the fish to steam for 10–15 minutes. Open foil and serve immediately.

Fish Parcels with Tomato and Basil SERVES 1

1 fish fillet (e.g. sea perch, blue
   grenadier, trevally, gemfish)
½ tomato, cut into slices
2 spring onions
black pepper to taste
a little freshly chopped basil or
   ¼–½ teaspoon dried basil

Cut out a large square piece of foil.
Place 2 slices of tomato on the
centre of the foil. Place fish on top.
Add more slices of tomato. Sprinkle
with chopped onions, black pepper
and lots of garden-fresh basil (or
dried basil). Fold up foil to
completely seal, and place on a hot
barbecue for about 10 minutes.

Alternatively, place 2 centimetres of
water in the base of a pan. Bring to
a simmer. Place foil parcels in
water, cover and leave the fish to
steam for approximately
10–15 minutes. Open foil and serve
immediately.

Fish Pâté SERVES 4–6

1 × 170 g can crab meat
1 × 210 g can red salmon
1 × 105 g can sardines
3 tablespoons Soymilk Mayonnaise
   (see page 51)
2 teaspoons gelatine
2 tablespoons boiling water
1 tablespoon lemon juice
lots of black pepper
finely chopped fresh chives for
   garnishing

Drain the cans of fish well, and
combine in a food processor with
the mayonnaise. Process until
smooth.

Dissolve gelatine in boiling water
and add lemon juice. Add this
slowly to the fish mixture while
machine is operating. Spoon into a
mould and refrigerate overnight.

To serve, unmould and press
chopped chives over the top.
Excellent with vegetable crudités or
wholemeal toast fingers.

Fish and Spinach Cannelloni

800 g–1 kg fish (e.g. sea perch,
whiting, flake)
12 sheets lasagne pasta (fresh or
instant variety)

**SPINACH AND RICOTTA
FILLING**
200 g spinach
200 g low-fat ricotta cheese
½ teaspoon ground nutmeg
½ teaspoon grated Parmesan
cheese

TOMATO SAUCE
1 onion, chopped
2 cloves garlic, crushed
2 × 400 g cans whole tomatoes in
natural juice, salt-free
½ cup tomato paste
½ teaspoon fresh basil
½ teaspoon dried oregano

Preheat oven to 180–200°C.

Prepare fish by removing skin and
bones, then cut into 12 pieces. Put
each piece between plastic and
gently roll out to approximately the
shape of the lasagne. If using instant
lasagne, cook sheets in boiling water
until just tender. Remove and drain.

To make the spinach and ricotta
filling, cook spinach, drain well and
finely chop. Combine with all other
filling ingredients.

For tomato sauce, cook onion and
garlic in a saucepan with a little
water until soft. Purée tomatoes in
juice, tomato paste and herbs and
add to onion and garlic. Slowly
bring to the boil. Turn down and
simmer for 5 minutes.

To assemble cannelloni, take a sheet
of cooked lasagne and top with one
piece of rolled-out fish. Place a
dessertspoon of the spinach and
ricotta across one end of the fish,
and roll up to encase the fish and
ricotta and spinach filling. Repeat
to make 12 cannelloni. Place in a
large casserole and pour the tomato
sauce on top. Cover with lid or
foil. Bake in oven for
45–55 minutes.

Serve two cannelloni per person,
with a salad.

Gemfish Pockets

2 gemfish fillets
200 g asparagus, steamed and
   lightly puréed

SAUCE
1 cup low-fat milk or low-fat
   soymilk
2 tablespoons cornflour
1 teaspoon wholegrain mustard
¼ teaspoon dry mustard
¼ teaspoon ground ginger

Cut a deep pocket in each fillet. Fill pockets with asparagus purée. If you have puréed asparagus to a smooth paste you may need to secure the pockets with toothpicks. Wrap fish in foil, place in a steamer and cover. Steam the fish pockets until fish is cooked through (about 10–15 minutes).

To make the sauce, mix a little milk in a saucepan with cornflour to make a paste. Add remaining ingredients, stirring well. Slowly bring to the boil, stirring until sauce thickens. Turn heat down. Cook a further couple of minutes, then pour over cooked fish just prior to serving.

Brown Rice Risotto with Prawns

SERVES 4

1 medium-sized onion, diced
1 teaspoon crushed garlic
1 teaspoon chopped fresh ginger
½ teaspoon cummin
¼ teaspoon chilli
½ teaspoon coriander
1 teaspoon olive oil
1 medium-sized green capsicum,
 thinly sliced
1 cup frozen peas
225 g low-grain brown rice,
 cooked
400–500 g shelled, deveined and
 cooked prawns
12 cherry tomatoes
freshly chopped coriander for
 garnishing (optional)

Cook onion, garlic, ginger, cummin, chilli and coriander in oil in a large pan until onion begins to soften and turn transparent. Add capsicum and peas and toss until vegetables are soft. Add rice, prawns and tomatoes. Toss to combine with vegetables. Cover for just a few minutes to heat evenly.

Garnish with freshly chopped coriander.

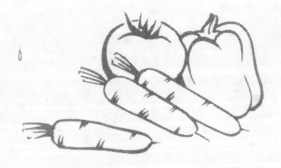

Curry Salmon Patties

350 g peeled potatoes
150 g carrots
220 g red salmon, drained
juice of ½ lemon
25 g low-fat grating cheese, grated
½–1 teaspoon curry powder
2 tablespoons finely chopped fresh
  parsley
2 tablespoons finely chopped spring
  onions (green part only)
1 egg white
2 tablespoons water
¾ cup wholemeal breadcrumbs
¼ cup oat bran

Preheat oven to 180°C.

Put potatoes and carrots in a saucepan, cover with water and cook until just tender. Drain and mash well.

Add salmon, lemon juice, cheese, curry, parsley and spring onions and mix well. Make 4 small patties.

Beat egg white and water together in a shallow dish. In another dish, combine the breadcrumbs and oat bran. Dip each patty into the egg mixture and roll in the breadcrumbs and oat bran.

Lightly oil a non-stick pan and brown patties on both sides for just a few minutes. Place patties on a lined baking tray and finish cooking in preheated oven for approximately 15–20 minutes.

JANUARY 2003

VERY GOOD COULD PUT A LITTLE MORE CURRY IN I PUT 1 TSP.

WE HAD RICE WITH IT SALAD AND VEG MIGHT BE NICE AS THIS RECIPE THOUGH TASTY IS A LITTLE DRY

Salmon and Ricotta Terrine

a few pieces finely chopped red
  capsicum
a few pieces finely chopped celery
finely chopped fresh herbs
  (optional)
½ teaspoon agar powder
½ cup unsweetened apple juice

TERRINE
1 × 440 can red salmon
250 g low-fat ricotta cheese
1 teaspoon wholegrain mustard
1 teaspoon hot English mustard
1 tablespoon tomato paste
1 tablespoon gelatine
1 tablespoon boiling water
2 tablespoons lemon juice
2 tablespoons finely chopped red
  capsicum
2 tablespoons finely chopped celery
black pepper to taste

Lightly oil the inside of a terrine
dish. Place the chopped vegetables
and/or fresh herbs on the base of
the dish (which will appear on the
top when the terrine is removed
from the dish).

Dissolve agar powder in apple juice
over heat and pour this over the
vegetables. Refrigerate until just set.

Blend salmon, ricotta, mustards and
tomato paste in a food processor
until smooth. Dissolve gelatine in
boiling water and add lemon juice.
Add this to the salmon and cheese
mixture. Fold in vegetables and add
black pepper. Spoon into the
prepared terrine dish and refrigerate
to set.

To unmould the terrine, sit the dish
for 5–10 seconds in a sink of hot
water that comes up to the top
edge of the dish. Turn dish upside
down on a platter, shake out the
terrine and cut into slices to serve.

Curried Scallop and Potato Pie

50 g diced onion
1 teaspoon crushed garlic
2 tablespoons water
2 teaspons curry powder
1 teaspoon cummin
2 teaspoons pink peppercorns
½ cup cornflour
3 cups low-fat milk or low-fat
  soymilk
1 cup sliced celery
1 cup fresh shelled peas
200 g carrots, cut into chunks
400 g scallops, cleaned
800 g peeled potatoes
2 bay leaves
extra low-fat milk

Combine onion, garlic, water, curry powder, cummin and peppercorns in a small saucepan and cook over a gentle heat with the lid on until onion is quite soft.

Combine cornflour with a little of the milk to make a paste. Stir in remaining milk. Pour over cooked onion and spices. Slowly bring to the boil, stirring continuously until sauce thickens. Cover and set aside.

Steam celery, peas and carrot until just tender and drain. While vegetables are cooking, place scallops in a dish and cover with boiling water. Place a lid on the dish and allow scallops to stand until they just change colour (approximately 1½–2 minutes). Drain well. Add vegetables and scallops to the sauce and place in a deep casserole dish.

Cook potatoes and bay leaves in water until potatoes are tender. Drain, remove leaves and mash potatoes with a little milk until smooth. For an attractive topping spoon the potato into a piping bag and pipe decoratively over the top of scallop and vegetable mixture.

When ready to cook, preheat oven to 180°C and bake for 40 minutes or until pie bubbles and potato is lightly browned on top.

Tuna and Vegetable Casserole

1 × 425 g can tuna
8 spring onions
500 g zucchini, cut into chunks
1 cup thinly sliced broccoli
1 cup thinly sliced cauliflower
1 cup diced carrot
½ cup diced red capsicum
½ cup diced green capsicum
(1 cup frozen peas can be
  substituted for red and green
  capsicum)

SAUCE
3 cups low-fat milk or low-fat
  soymilk
½ cup cornflour
1 teaspoon dried oregano
1 teaspoon dried basil
½ cup tomato paste

TOPPING
50 g low-fat grating cheese
½ cup oat bran
½ cup wholemeal or rye
  breadcrumbs
½ cup finely chopped fresh parsely

Preheat oven to 180°C.

Drain tuna and add onions. Steam zucchini, broccoli, cauliflower, carrot and capsicum until just tender and drain.

For the sauce, combine 1 cup of the milk with cornflour, herbs and tomato paste and mix well. Return this to remaining milk and heat in a small saucepan until sauce thickens. In a casserole dish combine tuna, onions and vegetables and add the sauce.

To make the topping, grate cheese and combine all ingredients. Spread evenly over the top of the casserole. Bake for 40 minutes or until bubbling and top is golden brown.

Excellent casserole to prepare a day ahead; just cover and refrigerate, uncooked. It will need a little more time in the oven if it goes straight from refrigerator to oven.

Tuna and Vegetable Croquettes

1 × 425 g can tuna
1 × 310 g can corn kernels or
  200 g fresh corn kernels, cooked
500 g potatoes, peeled, cooked
  and mashed
juice of 1 small lemon
100 g grated carrot
100 g grated zucchini (juice
  squeezed out)
100 g finely diced onion
3 egg whites
1 teaspoon dried dill
1 teaspoon fresh basil or
  ¼ teaspoon dried basil
black pepper to taste
½ cup oat bran

Preheat oven to 180°C.

Drain tuna and corn and combine with all other ingredients except oat bran. Mix well using your hands. Form into 12 small croquettes and roll lightly in oat bran. Refrigerate until firm before cooking.

Lightly oil a non-stick pan and cook croquettes for a few minutes on each side until light brown. Complete cooking by placing the croquettes on a lined baking tray and cooking for a further 15–20 minutes in preheated oven.

Sea Perch, Zucchini and Ginger Balls

SERVES 4–6

FISH BALLS
500 g sea perch
½ medium-sized onion, diced
150 g grated zucchini (juice
squeezed out)
1 teaspoon lemon juice
1 egg white
½ cup breadcrumbs

MARINADE
¼ cup apple juice concentrate
2 teaspoons finely chopped fresh
ginger
1 cup unsweetened orange juice
¾ cup dry sherry
1 tablespoon low-salt soy sauce
thin strips orange rind
2–3 tablespoons cornflour
2 tablespoons water

Place fish in a food processor and mince. Remove mince to a bowl, add all remaining fish ball ingredients and mix well using your hands. Shape into 8 or 12 balls.

Mix all marinade ingredients together. Put fish balls in marinade and marinate for at least 4–6 hours, turning twice.

When ready to cook preheat oven to 180°C.

Place fish balls in a shallow casserole with marinade liquid and cook in preheated oven for approximately 30–35 minutes or until fish is tender. Remove fish balls, set aside and cover.

Place marinade in a small saucepan. Mix cornflour and water to a paste. Stir this into marinade as it comes to the boil and stir until thickened. Pour sauce over the fish balls.

Seafood Fettuccine

400 g fresh fettuccine
1 medium-sized onion, diced
1 large clove garlic, crushed
¼ cup dry white wine
400 g clean fish or combination of prawns, scallops, fish, calamari, etc.
100 g spinach, cleaned and broken into small pieces
2½ cups low-fat milk or low-fat soymilk
¼ cup cornflour
2 teaspoons wholegrain mustard
½ teaspoon dry mustard

Drop fettuccine into a saucepan of rapidly boiling water. Cook until tender and drain.

While fettuccine is cooking place onion and garlic in a saucepan over low heat with the lid on. Cook for 2–3 minutes. Add wine and bring to the boil. Dice fish into bite-sized pieces and add to the saucepan. Turn heat down a little. Cover and cook fish until just tender. Add spinach and cover.

In a bowl mix a little of the milk with cornflour to make a paste. Add mustards and remaining milk. Pour this into the pan with the fish and gently stir continuously until sauce boils and thickens.

Place equal portions of fettuccine on 4 plates and top with the seafood and spinach sauce. Serve immediately.

Hawaiian Fish Kebabs

200 g trevally
4 wooden or steel kebab sticks
16 pieces green capsicum, about
   3 × 3 cm
8 pieces red capsicum, about
   3 × 3 cm
8 pieces fresh pineapple, about
   3 × 3 cm
8 small mushrooms

MARINADE
½ cup unsweetened pineapple juice
1 tablespoon lemon juice
1 teaspoon wholegrain mustard
1 teaspoon grated lemon rind

Make marinade by combining all ingredients in a bowl.

Cut fish into 16 pieces, each piece about 3 centimetres square. Thread fish, capsicum, pineapple and mushrooms onto kebab sticks. Place in marinade for 1 hour before ccoking, turning frequently.

To cook, steam the kebabs by covering them in their marinade and microwaving them for just a couple of minutes on both sides. Alternatively barbecue them, or cook them under a hot griller. They are cooked when the fish has turned very white.

When serving, the marinade can be thickened with a little cornflour to make a sauce to pour over the fish.

Opposite
Chicken Roll with Mustard Sauce (see page 75).

Eggplant and Mushroom Lasagne

450 g eggplant
1 small onion, chopped
1 teaspoon light olive oil
200 g thinly sliced mushroom
500 g grated carrot
2 × 400 g cans whole tomatoes in
   natural juice, salt-free
½ cup water or dry white wine
1 teaspoon dried dill
1 teaspoon ground cummin
1 teaspoon dried basil
black pepper to taste
1 × 140 g tub tomato paste
   (about 6 tablespoons)
½ red capsicum, diced
½ green capsicum, diced
1 × 250 g packet lasagne pasta,
   cooked

TOPPING
150 g low-fat grating cheese
1 cup rolled oats
a little paprika

Chop eggplant in a food processor or dice finely. Cook eggplant and onion in the oil until eggplant softens and begins to brown. Add the mushroom. Cover and continue cooking until mushroom has softened and changed colour. Stir frequently. Add carrot, tomatoes and juice, water or white wine, herbs and spices. Simmer for 20 minutes, covered. Add tomato paste and capsicum and cook a further 10 minutes.

Preheat oven to 200°C.

Place a layer of pasta on the base of a shallow casserole dish. Spoon one-third of the sauce over the top. Repeat with a further layer of pasta and another third of the sauce. Finally add another layer of pasta and remaining sauce.

For the topping, grate cheese and combine it with oats and paprika. Spread evenly over lasagne. Bake in preheated oven for 30–40 minutes, or until top is well browned. Serve with a salad.

Opposite
Fresh Fruit Custard Tart (see page 106).

Lima Bean Cannelloni

1 × 310 g can lima beans, drained
200 g spinach, cooked and well
   drained
50 g low-fat grating cheese
¼ teaspoon ground nutmeg
1 egg white
12 cannelloni shells

TOMATO SAUCE
1 small onion, diced
1 teaspoon crushed garlic
1 teaspoon light olive oil (optional)
6 large mushrooms, thinly sliced
½ cup red wine
1 × 400 g can whole tomatoes in
   natural juice, salt-free
2 tablespoons tomato paste

Rinse lima beans under cold water to remove salt. Chop spinach and add to beans. Grate cheese and add to bean mixture with nutmeg and egg white. Mix together. Spoon this mixture into the 12 cannelloni shells. Cover.

To make the tomato sauce, cook onion and garlic in the oil or a little water until onion is soft. Add sliced mushroom. Continue cooking until mushroom is soft. Add red wine. Chop up tomatoes and add with the juice. Mix in the tomato paste. Stir frequently and simmer for 20 minutes.

While sauce is cooking, preheat oven to 180°C. Place filled cannelloni shells in a lightly oiled baking dish. Pour the sauce over the top. Cover and bake in preheated oven for 30 minutes.

Serve with a salad.

Potato Bean Bake

1 onion, diced
1 teaspoon crushed garlic
100 g chopped celery
1 teaspoon curry powder
1 teaspoon garam masala
100 g diced carrot
1 cup frozen peas
1⅓ cups salt-free tomato juice
2 tablespoons tomato paste
400 g red kidney beans, cooked
½ cup finely chopped fresh parsley
700 g potatoes, peeled and sliced
  into thin rounds
100 g low-fat grating cheese, grated
a little paprika

Preheat oven to 200°C.

In a medium-sized non-stick pan cook onion, garlic, celery and spices until soft. Add carrot and peas with a little water and cover. Cook until carrot is tender. Add 1 cup of the tomato juice, tomato paste, beans and parsley. Cover and remove from heat.

Cook potato until just tender – not too soft. Drain. Place a layer of potato slices on the bottom of a rectangular casserole dish. Add bean and vegetable mixture. Overlap the remaining potato slices on top. Pour over remaining tomato juice. Sprinkle with cheese and a dash of paprika.

Cook in preheated oven for 30 minutes or until well browned on top.

Potato Corn Cakes

100 g low-fat grating cheese
3 large potatoes, peeled, cooked
   and mashed
1 cup rolled oats
1 cup corn kernels, cooked
black pepper to taste
2 tablespoons parsley

Grate cheese, combine all ingredients and make into 4 firm flat cakes. Refrigerate for 2 hours before cooking on a hot, lightly oiled surface. Turn and cook until both sides are browned.

Serve with a salad

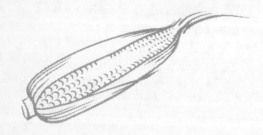

Curried Vegetables and Yoghurt Cucumber Dip

SERVES 2

a selection of the following
  (enough for 2 serves): broccoli,
  cauliflower, carrots, zucchini,
  squash, capsicum, Brussels
  sprouts, celery

YOGHURT CUCUMBER DIP
½ cup non-fat or low-fat yoghurt
¼ cup peeled, seeded and diced
  cucumber
a little crushed garlic (optional)
pinch of dried dill

CURRY SAUCE
1 teaspoon light olive oil or
  2 tablespoons water
½ onion, diced
1 teaspoon crushed garlic
1 teaspoon crushed fresh ginger
1 teaspoon turmeric
1 teaspoon ground coriander
1 teaspoon garam masala
1 teaspoon ground cummin
1 tablespoon water
1½ cups low-fat milk or low-fat
  soymilk
1 tablespoon cornflour

Cut broccoli and cauliflower into florets and cut each floret into 3 thin slices. Carrots can be cut diagonally into thin slices. Cut zucchini into julienne strips. Slice squash thinly. Cut capsicum into thin strips. Cut Brussels sprouts in half. Cut celery in Chinese-style diagonals. Steam chosen vegetables until just tender.

To make the yoghurt cucumber dip, combine all ingredients and refrigerate.

To make the curry sauce, place oil, onion and spices in a medium-sized saucepan. Stir over low heat until onion begins to soften. Add water to make a paste. Stir for 1 minute. Mix a little of the milk with the cornflour to make a paste. Stir it through remaining milk. Add to curry paste, stirring continuously until sauce simmers and thickens.

Add vegetables to sauce and coat well. Serve on a plate with brown rice and ¼ cup of yoghurt cucumber dip per person.

Low
Cholesterol
Desserts

Apples

'An apple a day keeps the doctor away' – it's not just a saying but a real message. There is nothing better than to crunch into a cold crispy apple. But do take care. Studies now show that the top and bottom cavities of apples harbour the build-up of chemical residue from sprays. It is best to remove there areas with a sharp knife before eating and thoroughly wash the skins as well.

Apple combinations taste great. Dice different varieties together and begin your day with a bowl of apples. Passionfruit pulp and diced pineapple also combine well with the taste of apples.

Bananas

These come in their own packaging, which makes them ideal to pack in the golf buggy, the hiker's back pack or the cyclist's back pocket for a quick energy boost.

For a fabulous, quick and easy, tasty ice-cream treat, just throw them in their skins into the freezer. When very firm, peel carefully and place in a food processor, then whip until smooth.

Banana Boys

Place whole bananas in the freezer for at least 24 hours to firm. Cut in half and remove peel. Insert a wooden stick in one end and chew away – or dip them into passionfruit pulp for extra flavour.

Banana Sesame Balls

Purée some frozen bananas, then fold in some finely chopped dates, shape into balls and roll in sesame seeds. Return to the freezer for a short time until firm.

Berries

Christmas holiday time usually instigates a trip to the local berry farm where blueberries, raspberries, strawberries, blackberries, loganberries and cranberries grow in abundance. The real pleasure in eating them is actually sitting under the berry bushes and indulging as you pick, or bringing them home and simply combining them all in a large bowl for a berry fruit salad.

Add some grated lemon or orange rind and a little fresh orange or pineapple juice to keep them moist, or a little champagne for a special occasion.

Fresh Fruit Salad

seasonal fruits, peeled and cut into bite-sized pieces
freshly chopped herbs (e.g. mint, sage, lemon balm, caraway seeds, coriander)
grated lemon rind
grated orange rind
grated fresh ginger (if using apple and pineapple)
dried fruits (e.g. figs, dates, nectarines, papaw, mango, apricots, peaches, pears)

WHIPPED RICOTTA CREAM
ricotta cheese
low-fat milk or low-fat soymilk
dash of vanilla essence or liqueur

Choose any combination of your favourite fruits in season and serve with non-fat or low-fat yoghurt, whipped ricotta cream or home-made ice-cream. To add flavour to your fruit salads try adding some freshly chopped herbs. Grated lemon and orange rind will give a tang, while grated fresh ginger goes well with apple and pineapple. Also try adding just a few slivers of dried fruits.

To make the ricotta cream, combine equal quantities of ricotta cheese and milk and purée for a thin running cream, or add a little less milk for a thicker consistency. Add a dash of vanilla essence to flavour or for a special taste add just a little of your favourite liqueur.

Jellied Fruit Salad

200 g fresh pineapple flesh
400 g fresh fruits (e.g. strawberries,
  kiwi fruit, peaches, oranges,
  passionfruit pulp)
2 cups cold water
2 tablespoons apple juice
  concentrate
(2 cups apple juice can be
  substituted for apple juice
  concentrate and water)
2 teaspoons agar powder

Chop up all fruit on a plate and reserve the fruit juices.

Place water and apple juice concentrate (or apple juice) and agar powder in a saucepan and slowly bring to the boil. Simmer, stirring until agar has dissolved. Cool slightly, then add the fruit juices and the fruit. Pour into a mould and refrigerate for at least 2–3 hours before serving.

Mango and Peach Jelly Log

2 mangoes, peeled
6 yellow peaches, peeled
2 passionfruit
1 cup freshly squeezed orange juice
1 cup water
1 teablespoon apple juice
  concentrate
2 teaspoons agar powder

Chop fruit into bite-sized pieces and add passionfruit pulp. Pour orange juice through a sieve to remove small fibres.

Combine water, apple juice concentrate and agar powder in a saucepan. Slowly bring to the boil, stirring continuously until agar dissolves. Remove from heat and add orange juice. Pour this over fruit immediately and spoon into a long, glass terrine-style dish. Refrigerate until firm, then cut into slices.

This fruit log keeps well if refrigerated and well covered.

Orange and Grapefruit Jelly

SERVES 4

150 g orange segments
150 g grapefruit segments
1 cup water
1 tablespoon apple juice
concentrate
1½ teaspoons agar powder
½ cup freshly squeezed orange
juice, strained

Remove any pips and pith from the fruit and save any juice.

Place water, apple juice concentrate and agar powder in a saucepan. Bring to the boil, then simmer for 3–5 minutes or until agar has dissolved. Stir in any reserved juice and add orange juice and fruit.

Pour into goblets or suitable jelly mould to set. Refrigerate until firm.

Pineapple Jelly Castle

SERVES 6–8

1 large pineapple (about 700 g
flesh)
1 cup water
1 tablespoon apple juice
concentrate
2 teaspoons agar powder
1 cup pineapple juice

Peel pineapple, remove core and dice flesh, saving any juices.

Place water, apple juice concentrate and agar powder in a saucepan. Bring to the boil, then simmer for 3–5 minutes or until agar has dissolved. Remove from heat. Add pineapple flesh, reserved juice and pineapple juice. Pour into a mould (if you don't own a castle-shaped jelly mould, any other shape will do) and refrigerate to set.

Home-made Vanilla Ice-cream

1 × 375 ml can low-fat evaporated skim milk
¼ cup apple juice concentrate
2 teaspoons vanilla essence
a little grated lemon rind

In a large bowl beat milk until thick and at least doubled in quantity. Add remaining ingredients while still beating. Pour into ice-cream maker and follow freezing instructions.

MAKING ICE-CREAM WITHOUT AN ICE-CREAM MAKER

- All ingredients used should be ice-cold.
- All equipment used should be well chilled. Place in freezer for at least 15 minutes prior to using.
- Pour ice-cream into well-chilled metal freezing containers.
- To avoid ice-cream texture becoming icy rather than creamy, you will need to rebeat it several times, just as icicles begin to appear around the edges again. Make sure that all equipment is well chilled.
- This ice-cream does not store well as it becomes rock hard. Make small batches and eat as required.
- Should ice-cream become too hard, place in a chilled blender or food processor and quickly blend to a creamy texture. Eat immediately.

VARIATION

- You can add 1 cup of fresh fruit of your choice to the above recipe (for example, mashed banana, puréed mango, sliced strawberries, blueberries or raspberries). Reduce the amount of apple juice concentrate when using very sweet fruits.

Apple and Pear Strudel

3 pears, peeled and thinly sliced
2 apples, peeled and thinly sliced
I egg white
I tablespoon apple juice
   concentrate
2 tablespoons water
2 tablespoons oat bran
8 sheets filo pastry
150 g dates, chopped
rind of I lemon
6 teaspoons lemon juice
ground cinnamon

Preheat oven to 180°C.

In separate pans, lightly cook pears and apples so that they remain firm and retain their shape.

Combine egg white, apple juice concentrate and water. Lay filo pastry on non-stick baking paper on a baking tray, layer on top of layer, wiping in between each second sheet of filo with the egg white and apple concentrate mixture, and sprinkling with a little of the oat bran.

In the centre of the pastry, leaving the edges uncovered to fold over later, make a layer of pear pieces. Top with half the dates. Add a layer of apple slices and remaining dates. Top with lemon rind and lemon juice.

Wipe the ends of the pastry with the egg white mixture and fold over the mixture. Wipe the sides with the egg white mixture and bring them up to almost touch, but leaving a little of the fruit mixture exposed. Wipe egg white mixture all over strudel. Sprinkle with remaining oat bran and shake the cinnamon over the top.

Cook in preheated oven for 15–20 minutes. Serve with Home-made Vanilla Ice-cream (see page 101).

Apple Oat Crumble

6–8 apples, peeled, cored and
quartered
1 cup unsweetened orange and
pineapple juice or orange juice
1 tablespoon cornflour
rind of 1 lemon
water

CRUMBLE TOPPING
100 g rolled oats
10 almonds
150 g egg whites (about 4 eggs)
1 teaspoon vanilla essence
2 tablespoons apple juice
concentrate

Preheat oven to 180°C.

Cook apples in the juice until
tender. Drain off liquid into a
saucepan and top up with water to
make 1 cup of liquid. Blend
cornflour with a little water and add
to the liquid in the pan. Add lemon
rind. Cook until sauce thickens,
stirring continuously. Place apples in
baking dish and pour the sauce over
the top. Leave to cool and set.

To make the crumble topping,
process rolled oats and almonds to a
breadcrumb texture. Beat egg
whites in a bowl until thick and
stiff. Add vanilla essence and apple
juice concentrate. Fold in oats and
almonds. Spread evenly over the set
apple. Cook in preheated oven for
20 minutes.

Serve with low-fat Home-made
Vanilla Ice-cream (see page 101) or
low-fat yoghurt.

Raspberry and Pear Summer Pudding

SERVES 6

800 g raspberries (fresh or frozen, not canned)
1 cup water
2 teaspoons agar powder
1 pear, peeled and thinly sliced
1 teaspoon grated lemon rind
10–12 slices oat bran bread (crusts removed)

Place raspberries, half of the water and agar powder in a saucepan and bring to the boil. Simmer for 3 minutes. Remove from heat. In the remaining water, cook the pear until soft, with the lemon rind. Drain well.

Use a medium-sized pudding basin and line with bread slices. Overlap the slices so there are no gaps. Pour half the raspberry mixture over the top. Top with bread slices (again, slightly overlapping) and firm down. Place a layer of pear slices over the bread. Pour remaining raspberries over the pears and top with more bread. Cover with plastic. Place a plate on top and a heavy weight. Refrigerate for at least 4–6 hours before serving.

Remove from pudding basin onto a plate. Cut into slices and serve decorated with fresh fruit, low-fat Home-made Vanilla Ice-cream (see page 101) or whipped ricotta cream (see page 98).

Banana Split

SERVES 1

1 banana
1 large scoop of Home-made Vanilla Ice-cream (see page 101)
4 dates, chopped
2 walnuts, chopped

Cut banana in half, lengthways. Top with ice-cream, dates and walnuts.

Berry Summer Jelly Pudding

800 g berries in season
   (e.g. strawberries, blueberries,
   raspberries, red currants,
   cherries)
4 cups water
4 teaspoons agar powder
1/4 cup apple juice concentrate

Clean berries, removing stems. Cut strawberries in half. Remove pips from cherries and cut in half.

Place water, agar and apple juice concentrate in a saucepan and bring to the boil. Simmer for 3–5 minutes or until agar is dissolved.

Turn up heat and add berries. Stir carefully. Bring nearly to the boil. Fruits will start to bleed their colours into the liquid and just begin to break open. Do not overcook them.

Remove from heat and pour into a round pudding bowl to set. Refrigerate to firm. Cut into wedges to serve.

Custard

2 cups low-fat milk or low-fat
   soymilk
1/4 cup cornflour
1 teaspoon vanilla essence
2 teaspoons orange rind
2–3 tablespoons apple juice
   concentrate

In a saucepan blend a little skim milk with cornflour to make a paste. Stir in remaining milk, vanilla and orange rind (the rind will give the liquid a lovely orange colour). Bring slowly to the boil, stirring continuously until custard begins to thicken. Cook over low heat for a further couple of minutes. Remove from heat. Stir in apple juice concentrate. (If you prefer a thinner custard, use a little more milk.)

Serve custard over stewed or fresh fruits, or the dessert of your choice. If custard is left to go cold it sets like a blancmange and can also be served as a cold dessert with Blueberry Sauce (see page 24).

Fresh Fruit Custard Tart

3 cups chopped fresh fruits
(e.g. banana, kiwi fruit,
strawberries, apricots, peaches,
pears) or 3 cups drained and
chopped unsweetened canned
fruits

PASTRY

1 cup unbleached wholemeal flour
1 cup rolled oats
¼ cup cold pressed grapeseed oil
2 tablespoons apple juice
concentrate
2–4 tablespoons unsweetened
orange juice or lemon juice

CUSTARD

2 cups low-fat milk or low-fat
soymilk
½ cup cornflour
1 teaspoon vanilla essence
1 tablespoon grated orange rind
2–3 tablespoons apple juice
concentrate
½–1 cup non-fat or low-fat
yoghurt

GLAZE

1 tablespoon sugar-free raspberry
fruit spread
1 cup water
1 teaspoon agar powder

Preheat oven to 210°C.

To make pastry, combine all
ingredients in a food processor.
Using the steel blade, process until
pastry binds together. Knead lightly.
Roll pastry out to fit a fluted pie
dish. Place the pastry in the dish,
trim the edges and bake in
preheated oven for 10–15 minutes.
Remove from dish and cool.

To make custard, bring 1½ cups of
the milk to just below boiling point
in a medium-sized saucepan.
Combine rest of milk with the
cornflour, vanilla and orange rind to
make a paste. Add this to the hot
milk and stir briskly until thick.
Cook for 2 minutes, stirring
continuously. Remove from heat.
Add apple juice concentrate, mix
well, and then add yoghurt. Pour
into cooled pastry shell, and add the
chopped fruits.

To make glaze, place all ingredients
in a saucepan and bring to the boil,
stirring continuously. Simmer for
6 minutes, uncovered. Cool slightly
and brush over fruits. Cool before
serving.

Bread Pudding

4 large slices oat bran bread

4 large tablespoons sugar-free
   raspberry jam or plum jam

¾ cup currants

1 cup low-fat milk or low-fat
   soymilk

1 tablespoon cornflour

1 tablespoon apple juice
   concentrate

2 teaspoons vanilla essence

2 egg whites

Preheat oven to 180°C.

Lightly oil a deep rectangular baking dish or cake tin. The size of the tin should accommodate 2 slices of bread side by side. Spread 2 slices of bread with the jam. Place bread on the base of tin. Sprinkle with half the currants. Top with remaining bread slices and currants.

Combine a little milk with the cornflour to make a paste and stir it into remaining milk. Add apple juice concentrate and vanilla. Beat egg whites until firm and fold into the milk mixture. Pour this over the bread.

Cook in preheated oven for 30 minutes. Serve with Custard (see page 105).

Pineapple Pie

1¼ cups oat bran
1½ cups unbleached white flour
1 teaspoon baking powder
  (optional)
2 teaspoons grated lemon rind
⅓ cup cold pressed grapeseed oil
2 tablespoons apple juice
  concentrate
¼ cup lemon juice
¼ cup water

FILLING

2 cups fresh orange juice or
  unsweetened orange juice
1 tablespoon orange-flavoured
  liqueur (e.g. Galliano, Grand
  Marnier)
1 tablespoon grated orange rind or
  lemon rind
500–600 g fresh pineapple pieces
¼ cup cornflour

Preheat oven to 200°C.

Combine oat bran, flour, baking powder (if using, this addition makes a 'cakier' pastry) and lemon rind in a bowl and mix well.

Combine oil, apple juice concentrate and lemon juice and add this to the flour mixture and work through. Add enough water to make a firm dough. Knead and roll out to fit a fluted metal pie dish. Bake in preheated oven for 12–15 minutes. Remove and cool.

To make filling, combine 1½ cups of the orange juice with the liqueur and orange rind in a saucepan. As the liquid begins to simmer, add pineapple pieces. Blend cornflour with remaining juice and add, stirring until sauce thickens. Cool slightly before pouring into cooled pie shell. Refrigerate for at least 4–6 hours before serving.

Oat Bran
Bread and
Breadmaking

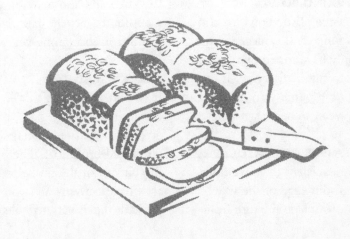

Breadmaking

These oat bran bread recipes, both savoury and sweet, have been developed to give you a good intake of oat bran in your daily diet, as well as the pleasure of baking your own bread. The oat bran content gives the breads a heavy texture and a nutty flavour that complements their fruit and vegetable content. The recipes are very simple to follow and each makes approximately a one-kilogram loaf.

These recipes have been made with the help of a large bread dough hook on a large capacity food mixer, but you can still make the breads using only your hands. It just means lots of hand kneading to get good results.

You can also substitute wholemeal flour for unbleached white flour, but the end result will be a little heavier. (To avoid this you could add just a little more yeast and some extra liquid.)

Equipment for breadmaking

LARGE MIXING BOWL
I use the large plastic bowl from my large food mixer. It is ideal because it can easily be warmed by running under hot water and drying. It then seems to hold in the warmth, which helps the yeast to begin working.

METAL KNIVES OR SPATULAS
These are excellent to move flour away from the edge of the bowl. Use them to scrape mixture from the bowl and also to work it on a well-floured bench. This saves hands from becoming very sticky.

BLACK BREAD TIN
It is worth investing in a 'real' bread tin with high sides that will give you a loaf resembling a purchased bread loaf. The black on the outside of the tin helps it to absorb heat evenly and you will end up with much better results. When

you first purchase your black bread tin you need to rub the inside liberally with oil. Wipe off the excess oil with a tissue. Place in a very hot oven (220°C) for approximately 15 minutes, then remove and leave to cool. When you are ready to bake the bread you simply lightly oil the tin again. This prevents the bread from sticking to the sides and gives a crusty finish. The bread should fall out of the tin when it is cooked.

LARGE FOOD MIXER

This is optional, but if you are a keen bread maker without a lot of time for hard kneading the mixer certainly takes the hassle out of breadmaking. Generally you operate the machine on a low speed for about 7 minutes. If you are making bread by hand, you will need to knead the dough for a similar time. The dough is ready when it becomes firmer and has a smooth texture.

Ingredients for breadmaking

UNBLEACHED WHITE BREAD FLOUR

This is a pure white flour with the bran and husks removed, but without chemicals or additives.

UNBLEACHED WHOLEMEAL FLOUR

This is a highly nutritious flour with all the husks from the wheat included. For the best results use a good quality fresh flour.

YEAST

There are different yeasts on the market and some have very 'yeasty' smells and tastes. One of the best I have used is Fermipan, which is available at supermarkets.

APPLE JUICE CONCENTRATE

This is used as a sweetener. It contains one third of the calories of refined sugar and honey, and as it is made from apples, the pectin in it is an excellent source of fibre. The natural sugar helps the yeast to grow.

CALCIUM ASCORBATE

This is used as a bread improver. It will increase the shelf life of the bread. It does not alter the flavour and is an optional addition.

COLD PRESSED GRAPESEED OIL

This is a cholesterol-free polyunsaturated oil that has been extracted with little or no heat or use of chemicals and solvents. In this process the vitamin E content is not destroyed.

LIQUID

In most recipes I have used very warm water, but you could use low-fat milk or low-fat soymilk as long as they are heated to a very warm temperature, without boiling.

Basic breadmaking instructions

flour
oat bran
yeast
calcium ascorbate
fruits, vegetables, nuts, cheese, etc.
  (if using)
oil
apple juice concentrate
very warm water

Place flour, oat bran, yeast and calcium ascorbate in a large mixing bowl. Mix to combine ingredients. At this point add fruits, vegetables, nuts, cheese, etc., as specified in the recipe, but make sure they have been brought to room temperature (if they have come directly from the fridge they will be cold and will delay the working of the yeast).

Add oil and apple juice concentrate and pour in the very warm water. Use a knife to scrape the flour away from the sides of the bowl and turn it back into the centre.

Mix in a food mixer (using bread dough hook) on low speed for approximately 6–7 minutes, or mix as much as possible with the knife, then turn the dough out onto a floured bench (use only unbleached white flour) and begin kneading.

The longer you knead, the better the end result will be.

If mixing in a food mixer, turn dough out onto a floured bench and knead to make a good firm shape. The bread will be firm but sticky when it leaves the bowl.

Cut the dough into 2 equal parts and drop both into a bread tin, each in one half of the tin. This will give your bread the traditional, double, high tin appearance, or make a log shape and drop into the tin.

You can brush the top of the dough with water, skim milk or diluted soymilk and sprinkle with poppyseeds, sesame seeds, cracked wheat, caraway seeds or spices.

Leave in a warm place (a prewarmed oven that has been turned off is excellent, or near a heater, or in a car that is parked in the sun) and leave until the dough reaches the top of the tin (approximately 30 minutes).

To cook, place the dough in a hot oven (220–230°C) and cook for approximately 30 minutes. The bread is cooked when the loaf sounds hollow when tapped.

Basic Oat Bran Bread

MAKES I LOAF

2 cups unbleached white flour
1½ cups oat bran
I tablespoon yeast
2 teaspoons calcium ascorbate
I tablespoon cold pressed
  grapeseed oil
I tablespoon apple juice
  concentrate
1½ cups very warm water or
  low-fat milk, or ¾ cup low-fat
  soymilk

Follow basic breadmaking
instructions (see page 113).

Make sure the loaf is completely
cold before slicing. If you use an
electric knife to slice this bread you
can make excellent wholesome
sandwiches – or slice it thick for
crunchy toast.

Apple and Lemon
Oat Bran Bread

MAKES I LOAF

2 cups unbleached white flour
1½ cups oat bran
2 teaspoons calcium ascorbate
I tablespoon yeast
I tablespoon cold pressed
  grapeseed oil
I tablespoon apple juice
  concentrate
1½ cups very warm water
½ cup grated apple, firmly packed
  (juice squeezed out before
  measuring)
I tablespoon finely grated lemon
  rind
I teaspoon mixed spice

(This is a moist bread with a light
lemony flavour from the addition of
lemon rind.)

To make this loaf, follow the basic
breadmaking instructions
(see page 113).

Banana and Walnut
Oat Bran Bread

MAKES I LOAF

2 cups unbleached white flour
1½ cups oat bran
2 teaspoons calcium ascorbate
1 tablespoon yeast
1 tablespoon cold pressed
  grapeseed oil
1 tablespoon apple juice
  concentrate
1½ cups very warm water
½ cup mashed banana
¼ cup walnuts, chopped

(This loaf smells absolutely
wonderful as you take it from the
oven and you'll be tempted to cut
it immediately, but remember that
hot bread does not slice very well,
so it's best to leave it stand a good
hour before slicing. It makes
delicious lettuce and banana
sandwiches or banana and alfalfa
sprout sandwiches, or just top it
with low-fat cottage cheese.)

To make the loaf, follow the basic
breadmaking instructions
(see page 113).

Cheese, Celery and Pecan Oat Bran Bread

2 cups unbleached wholemeal flour
1½ cups oat bran
1 tablespoon yeast
2 teaspoons calcium ascorbate
½ cup finely diced celery
¼ cup pecan nuts, finely chopped
½ cup grated low-fat grating
  cheese, firmly packed
1 tablespoon cold pressed
  grapeseed oil
1 tablespoon apple juice
  concentrate
1½ cups very warm water

(This is an excellent bread for pâté. It keeps its moisture and its flavours develop with time.)

Place the dry ingredients in a bowl, add the cheese and mix through, using your hands. Then follow the basic breadmaking instructions (see page 113).

Fruit Oat Bran Bread

2 cups unbleached wholemeal flour
1½ cups oat bran
1 tablespoon yeast
2 teaspoons calcium ascorbate
1 teaspoon ground cinnamon
1 teaspoon mixed spice
1 teaspoon ground nutmeg
1½ cups chopped dried fruits
(e.g. peaches, nectarines, pears,
dates, raisins, sultanas, mixed
peel)

2 tablespoons apple juice
concentrate
1 tablespoon cold pressed
grapeseed oil
1½ cups very warm water
1 tablespoon poppyseeds

To make this loaf, follow the basic breadmaking instructions (see page 113). Brush the top with low-fat milk or water and sprinkle with poppyseeds.

Onion, Garlic and Sesame Oat Bran Bread

1 medium-sized onion, diced
2 cloves garlic, crushed (optional)
1 tablespoon sesame seeds
2 cups unbleached white flour
1½ cups oat bran
1 tablespoon yeast
2 teaspoons calcium ascorbate
1 tablespoon cold pressed
grapeseed oil
1 tablespoon apple juice
concentrate
1½ cups very warm water
extra sesame seeds or poppyseeds

Place onion, garlic and sesame seeds in a small saucepan. Cover and cook on a low heat until garlic and onion are very soft. Then follow the basic breadmaking instructions (see page 113), adding the slightly cooked onion and garlic after the warm water.

Place in tin, brush top with water and sprinkle with sesame or poppyseeds.

Potato, Dill and Caraway Oat Bran Bread

½ cup grated potato, firmly packed
2 cups unbleached white flour
1½ cups oat bran
I tablespoon yeast
2 teaspoons calcium ascorbate
2 teaspoons dried dill
I tablespoon cold pressed
   grapeseed oil
I tablespoon apple juice
   concentrate
1½ cups very warm water
2 tablespoons sunflower seeds
caraway seeds

Squeeze moisture out of the grated potato. Run under cold water to remove starch and squeeze out all moisture again. Then follow the basic breadmaking instructions (see page 113).

Brush the top of the finished dough with water and sprinkle with caraway seeds.

Raisin Oat Bran Bread

2 cups unbleached white flour
1½ cups oat bran
1 tablespoon yeast
2 teaspoons calcium ascorbate
2 teaspoons mixed spice
½ teaspoon ground cinnamon
½ teaspoon ground nutmeg
1 tablespoon finely grated orange
rind
1½ cups raisins
2 tablespoons apple juice
concentrate
1 tablespoon cold pressed
grapeseed oil
1½ cups very warm water

(This loaf develops in flavour as it keeps – that is, if you can keep it! It also makes great toast.)

To make the loaf, follow the basic breadmaking instructions (see page 113).

Where do you find cholesterol and fats?

Key to symbols in table

- Negligible
0 Nil
ND No data available
Depends on type of fat used

s Salt added during processing
s* Salt added during processing. No Added Salt varieties also avilable
SR Reduced-salt varieties available; in other words, less than usual amounts of salt added

	Mass	Weight	Kilojoules	Calories	Fat content (g)	Saturated fat (g)	Cholesterol (mg)
Beef							
Hamburger mince, raw	1 serve	125g	1155	275	20	9	90
Rump steak, raw, lean only	1 small piece	125g	555	130	3	1	85
Silverside, roast, lean and fat	3 slices	90g	870	210	11	5	75
Silverside, corned, lean only	2 slices	60g	325	80	2	1	45
Veal, roast, lean and fat	3 slices	90g	535	130	1	1	100
Veal, schnitzel, raw, lean only	1 small piece	100g	460	110	2	1	80
Biscuits							
Savoury (e.g. Sao) (SR)	2	18g	330	80	3	1–2	#
Crispbread (s*)	2	16g	210	50	1	1	0
Sweet plain (e.g. Marie, Milk Arrowroot) (s)	2	18g	320	75	2	1	ND
Rich sweet (e.g. shortbread, butter biscuits) (s)	2	37g	755	180	9	2–5	ND
Sweet cream (s)	2	38g	775	185	9	2–5	ND
Choc. coated, cream filled (s)	2	36g	575	140	6	1–4	ND
Choc. coated (s)	2	29g	575	140	6	4	ND

	Mass	Weight	Kilojoules	Calories	Fat content (g)	Saturated fat (g)	Cholesterol (mg)
Breads, Pasta & Cereals							
Bread (s*R)	1 slice	30g	285	65	1	—	0
Bread rolls (s*R)	1	60g	740	175	3	—	0
Pitta	1 small	25g	300	70	1	—	0
Rolled oats, cooked	1 cup	250g	465	110	2	—	0
Rice, pasta, cooked	½ cup	75g	380	90	—	—	0
Breakfast cereals (e.g. Cornflakes, Weet-Bix) (s*R)	1 cup	30g	465	110	—	—	0
Muesli, toasted (s*)	¼ cup	30g	555	130	6	2	0
Muesli, untoasted (s*)	¼ cup	30g	460	110	3	1	0
Unprocessed bran	1 tablespoon	5g	40	10	—	0	0
Wheatgerm	1 tablespoon	7g	105	25	1	—	0
Cakes, Pastries							
Baklava, Lebanese (s)	1 slice	50g	540	245	18	10	25
Cake, plain (e.g. madeira) (s)	1 slice	60g	990	235	10	1–6	ND
Cake, rich fruit (s)	1 slice	60g	840	200	7	1–4	30
Cake, fancy iced (s)	1 slice	60g	1030	245	9	2–5	ND
Cheesecake (s)	⅛ of 20cm cake	120g	2095	505	42	#	115
Fruit pie, pastry top and bottom (s)	⅛ of 20cm pie	140g	2175	515	22	4–13	ND
Confectionery							
Butterscotch (s)	5	25g	440	105	2	1	ND
Boiled lollies	5	25g	350	81	—	0	—
Chocolate, plain milk (s)	10 small squares	50g	1105	265	15	9	45

	Mass	Weight	Kilojoules	Calories	Fat content (g)	Saturated fat (g)	Cholesterol (mg)
Fruit and coconut bars (e.g. apricot and coconut) (s)	1	40g	535	125	7	5	ND
Marshmallow, plain	5	25g	340	80	–	0	–
Novelty chocolate bars (s) (e.g. Picnic, Cherry Ripe, Flake, Caramel Whip)	1	50g	955	225	10	6	ND
Dairy Foods							
Cheese, cheddar (SR)	1 packaged slice	20g	335	80	7	4	15
Cheese, creamed cottage (s*)	1 tablespoon	20g	85	20	1	1	–
Cheese, med. fat¹ (e.g. ricotta, Cotto) (s*R)	1 tablespoon	20g	140	35	3	2	ND
Cheese, cream (s)	1 tablespoon	20g	285	68	7	4	20
Cream, whipping	1 tablespoon	20g	275	65	7	4	20
Ice-cream	2 scoops	60g	420	100	2	1	15
Milk, full cream	1 cup	250ml	700	165	10	6	35
Milk, fat reduced (e.g. Rev, Hilo)	1 cup	250ml	620	150	6	4	20
Milk, skim	1 cup	250ml	365	85	–	0	5
Milk, goat's	1 cup	250ml	760	180	12	8	ND
Buttermilk²	1 cup	250ml	505	120	5	3	ND
Yoghurt, full cream, plain	1 carton	200g	660	160	7	4	35
Yoghurt, full cream, flavoured	1 carton	200g	830	200	7	4	35
Yoghurt, non fat, plain	1 carton	200g	560	135	–	0	–
Yoghurt, non fat, flavoured	1 carton	200g	685	165	–	0	–

Mass		Weight	Kilojoules	Calories	Fat content (g)	Saturated fat (g)	Cholesterol (mg)
Drinks, Alcoholic							
Beer	1 can	370ml	590	140	0	0	0
Beer, alcohol reduced 2.2%	1 can	370ml	440	105	0	0	0
Beer, alcohol reduced, 0.9–1%	1 can	370ml	315	75	0	0	0
Liqueur, average	1 liqueur glass	20ml	230	55	0	0	0
Sherry, sweet	1 small glass	60ml	335	80	0	0	0
Sherry, dry	1 small glass	60ml	290	70	0	0	0
Spirits	1 nip	30ml	290	70	0	0	0
Wine, sweet or dry, average	1 glass	120ml	400	95	0	0	0
Drinks							
Fruit juice see Fruits							
Fruit juice drinks	1 carton	250ml	420	100	1	0	0
Milkshake	1 container	370ml	1360	325	13	8	55
Soft drinks, low kilojoule (s)	1 can	370ml	0	0	0	0	0
Soft drinks, cider	1 can	370ml	685	165	0	0	0
Tea, coffee (black)	1 can	250ml	0	0	0	0	0
Eggs							
Whole	1 med.	55g	335	80	6	2	250
Fats, Oils, Dressings							
Butter (s*R)	1 tablespoon	19g	580	140	16	10	45
Copha	1 tablespoon	17g	625	150	17	15	0

Mass	Weight	Kilojoules	Calories	Fat content (g)	Saturated fat (g)	Cholesterol (mg)
Dripping, lard	1 tablespoon	17g	625	150	17	14	25
Margarine, cooking (s)	1 tablespoon	19g	550	130	15	6	20
Margarine, polyunsaturated (s*R)	1 tablespoon	19g	580	140	15	3	5
Margarine, table (s)	1 tablespoon	19g	565	135	15	6	5
Mayonnaise, polyunsaturated (s)	1 tablespoon	19g	385	90	9	1	5
Mayonnaise, reg. (s)	1 tablespoon	19g	95	20	2	—	5
Oil, olive	1 tablespoon	18g	660	160	18	3	0
Oil, peanut	1 tablespoon	18g	660	160	18	4	0
Oil, polyunsaturated (e.g. saff, sun, soya, maize, cottonseed)	1 tablespoon	18g	660	160	18	3	0
Salad dressing (e.g. French, Italian) (s)	1 tablespoon	19g	285	70	7	1	0
Salad dressing, low joule, no oil (s)	1 tablespoon	19g	20	5	—	—	0
Solid cooking fat (e.g. Supa-Fry, Frymaster, Hi-Fri)	1 tablespoon	18g	625	150	17	8	30
Fruits						
Fresh	av. serve	100g	190	45	—	0	0
Canned or stewed, sweetened	¾ cup	180g	500	120	—	0	0
Canned or stewed, no added sugar	¾ cup	180g	200	50	—	0	0
Dried	6 pieces	30g	315	75	—	0	0
Juice, unsweetened	1 glass	150ml	225	55	—	0	0
Juice, sweetened	1 glass	150ml	285	65	—	0	0
Avocado, stone removed	½ med.	100g	920	220	22	3	0
Olives, with pips (s)	6 med.	30g	100	25	3	1	0
Sultanas	1 tablespoon	15g	160	40	—	0	0

	Mass	Weight	Kilojoules	Calories	Fat content (g)	Saturated fat (g)	Cholesterol (mg)
Game							
Rabbit	no accurate Australian figures available						
Venison	no accurate Australian figures available						
Lamb							
Roast leg, lean meat only	3 slices	90g	665	160	5	3	100
Chump chops, grilled, lean and fat	2 chops	170g	1985	475	31	17	185
Chump chops, grilled, lean only	2 chops	150g	1250	300	12	7	160
Miscellaneous							
Non-dairy whitener	2 heaped teaspoons	8g	180	45	3	3	ND
Sugar	1 rounded teaspoon	8g	130	30	0	0	0
Nuts							
Almonds	30	30g	710	170	16	1	0
Cashew	15	30g	670	160	14	3	0
Coconut, fresh	(5×2.5×1cm)	30g	435	105	11	9	0
Coconut, desiccated	¼ cup	25g	625	150	16	13	0
Macadamia	20	30g	940	225	23	4	0
Peanuts	40	30g	710	170	15	2	0
Pecans	20 halves	30g	895	215	21	2	0
Pine nuts	1½ tablespoons	30g	730	175	15	2	0
Walnuts	15 halves	30g	670	160	16	2	0

Mass	Weight	Kilojoules	Calories	Fat content (g)	Saturated fat (g)	Cholesterol (mg)
Offal						
Brains, steamed	1 set	90g	510	120	8	3	1695
Kidney, veal, raw	100g	450	105	4	2	270
Liver, beef, raw	100g	655	155	9	4	270
Tongue, boiled	med. serve	90g	1160	280	23	12	95
Pork						
Leg steak, raw, lean only	av. serve	125g	545	130	2	1	70
Loin chop, raw, lean and fat	1 chop	190g	2250	540	50	19	95
Roast leg, lean meat only	3 slices	90g	650	155	4	1	85
Bacon, grilled, lean and fat (s)	2 small rashers	30g	520	125	11	5	20
Ham, canned, lean (SR)	2 slices	60g	300	70	3	1	20
Poultry						
Chicken, breast, raw, lean only	½ breast	150g	705	170	3	1	75
Chicken, leg, roast, with skin	2 drumsticks (+ bone)	220g	1255	300	19	6	190
Duck, roast, meat only	3 slices	90g	710	170	9	3	145
Duck, roast, meat and skin	2 slices	90g	1265	305	26	8	145
Turkey, roast, meat only	3 slices	90g	530	125	2	1	75
Sauces and Spreads						
Honey, jam	1 tablespoon	27g	365	85	0	0	0
Peanut butter (s*)	1 tablespoon	20g	520	125	11	2	0

	Mass	Weight	Kilojoules	Calories	Fat content (g)	Saturated fat (g)	Cholesterol (mg)
Soy sauce (s*)	few drops	2g	0	0	0	0	0
Tomato sauce (s*)	1 tablespoon	21g	90	20	—	0	0
Vegemite, Marmite (s)	1 teaspoon	5g	40	10	—	0	0
Seafood							
Calamari, raw	med. serve	100g	ND	ND	1	—	190
Crab, canned, cooked, meat only (s)	¾ cup	75g	255	50	1	—	65
Fish, cooked	1 fillet	120g	460	110	2	—	70
Lobster, cooked, meat only	½ cup	100g	500	120	3	—	150
Mussels, fresh, meat only	6 large	60g	220	50	1	—	30
Oysters, raw, meat only	6 med.	60g	130	30	—	—	30
Prawns, cooked, meat only	6 king prawns	65g	295	70	1	—	130
Salmon, canned (s*)	½ med. can	110g	590	145	6	2	50
Salmon, smoked (s)	2 slices	30g	180	45	1	—	20
Sardines, canned in oil, drained (s*)	3 small	30g	270	65	4	1	30
Sardines, canned in oil, not drained (s*)	2–3 small	30g	415	100	9	2	25
Scallops, steamed, meat only	6 med.	60g	265	65	1	—	25
Tuna, canned in oil (s*)	½ med. can	110g	1320	320	24	7	70
Tuna, canned in water, or brine (s)	½ med. can	110g	525	125	3	1	ND
Smallgoods							
Devon, Fritz (s)	2 slices	50g	500	120	10	4	25
Frankfurters, saveloys, boiled (s)	2 med.	100g	1040	250	20	8	60
Salami (s)	4 thin slices	40g	720	170	15	6	40

	Mass	Weight	Kilojoules	Calories	Fat content (g)	Saturated fat (g)	Cholesterol (mg)
Sausages, beef, grilled or fried (s)	2 thick	140g	1560	375	18	8	60
Sausages, pork, grilled or fried (s)	2 thick	140g	1845	440	34	15	75
Snack Foods							
Packet snacks (s) (e.g. Twisties, Cheezels)	1 small packet	25g	525	125	7	3	—
Potato crisps (s*R)	1 small packet	25g	545	130	8	4	—
Popcorn, popped, plain	1 cup	15g	240	60	—	—	0
Pretzels (s)	1 small packet	50g	800	190	4	1	0
Take-aways							
BBQ chicken, meat, skin and fat (s)	¼ (drumstick & thigh)	100g	1030	245	15	5	100
Chicken, crumbed and fried (s)	¼ (drumstick & thigh)	130g	1795	430	28	8–12	100
Chinese, chicken and almond (s)	1 large serve	500g	2880	685	50	18	230
Chinese, prawn cutlets (s)	1 av. serve	200g	2200	525	30	5	330
Chips (s*)	av. commercial serve	200g	2190	520	30	11	20
Fish, fried in batter (s)	1 piece	150g	1600	380	24	5–14	40
Fried rice (s)	small container	200g	1860	440	17	3–8	60
Hamburger, plain (s)	1	170g	1610	385	17	7	45
Lebanese, homous (s)	1 serve	160g	1520	360	27	3	0
Lebanese, shish kebab (s)	3 sticks	200g	1585	380	20	10	270
Meat pie (s)	1	170g	1625	390	23	11	35

	Mass	Weight	Kilojoules	Calories	Fat content (g)	Saturated fat (g)	Cholesterol (mg)
Pizza, average (s)	reg. commercial	460g	5025	1195	52	23	85
Potato scallop (s)	1	100g	1360	325	22	12	20
Sausage roll (s)	1	130g	1580	375	25	12	25
Spring roll, fried (s)	1	175g	1695	405	17	8	20
Vegetables							
Potato, boiled or baked in jacket	1 med.	100g	345	80	—	0	0
Potato, roast	½ med.	70g	465	110	3	1	#
Potato, hot chips see Take-aways							
Potato, mashed, milk and fat added	½ cup	100g	500	120	5	3	#
Legumes/lentils (except soya beans), cooked	½ cup	100g	400	95	—	—	0
Soya beans, cooked	½ cup	100g	485	115	5	1	0
Starchy vegetables (e.g. baked beans, corn, parsnip, peas)	½ cup	100g	260	60	—	0	0
Other vegetables	av. serve	100g	40—	10—	—	0	0

Taken from the National Heart Foundation's booklet *Planning Fat-Controlled Meals*, with its kind permission.
[1] Low-fat ricotta also available.
[2] Some States negligible fat.

Where do you find cholesterol and fats?   **129**

Index